"Bitch!"
The Autobiography of
Lady Lawford
as told to Buddy Galon
with an Introduction by
Prince Franz Hohenlohe

Library of Congress Cataloging-in-Publication Data

Lawford, May, Lady, d. 1972.
  Bitch:the autobiography of Lady Lawford.
  Includes index.
  1. Lawford, May, Lady, d. 1972. 2. United Sates -
Biography. 3. Great Britain - Biography. 4. Actresses -
Great Britain - Biography. 5. Kennedy family. I. Galon,
Buddy. II. Title.
CT275.L2778A35 1986   973.922'092'4[B] 85-29116
ISBN 0-8283-1995-2

Branden Publishing Company
17 Station Street Box 843
Brookline Village MA 02147

Dedication

To my grandchildren:
Christopher Kennedy Lawford
Sydney Lawford
Victoria Francis Lawford
Robin Elizabeth Lawford

Once when you were very young, you said, "We already have a grandmother. Her name is Rose. She is very beautiful and very rich and has five houses. Thank you very much, but we don't want another grandmother."

My darling children, I too am your grandmother, and I do love you.

Lady Lawford

Acknowledgment

To the ladies of my life— Eleanor Powell, Beulah Bondi, Adela Rogers St. John, Lori Lane, Thelma Keaton, Zee Gee Jordan, and Chris Noel— for your love, your guidance, your understanding, and your encouragement of me and all of my endeavors, I bow lowly to each of you in deep affection.

To the gentlemen of my life— Prince Franz Hohenlohe, Patrick Mahony, Richard Brian, Peter Dane, Dr. Richard Mazurek, Dr. Leon Thomas, and Richard Fielden— for your honorableness, your courtesy, your loyalty, and your support, I shake your hand thanking each of you for your warm friendship.

Buddy Galon

Table of Contents

"Bitch!"
The Autobigraphy
of
Lady Lawford

Introduction

By Prince Franz   Hohenlohe

Not so many years ago, the *Reader's Digest* ran a series to which its subscribers were invited to contribute. If my memory serves, I believe it was called "The most unforgettable character I ever met". It did not occur to me at the time to send in an entry; but, had I done so, my choice would have been one very formidable lady (or should I spell it Lady?) whose Christian name was May. I should have called my article "My friend May".

She was the strong-willed mother of the late Peter Lawford; wife of a very distinguished man of the old school, General Sir Sydney Lawford; and she, of course, was Lady Lawford.

When I first knew May, her son Peter's movie career was at its zenith and May basked in all its reflected glory. The Lawfords had a lovely house on Sunset Boulevard and entertained there generously. Since Sir Sydney was a most likeable man, Peter a good looking bachelor, and May a gay little bird of a hostess, their home never lacked for friends who dropped in most afternoons.

I knew, like all of us did, that before Peter was put under contract by Louis B. Mayer, things had not always been so easy for that small British family, so far removed from England and the life they had known before the war. At first, when the three arrived from Europe, one of their well-heeled social friends lent them his house in Florida. May would sit on the private beach every day, doing her knitting for British war relief.

But soon she found that others, whom she did not see and who did not see her— hidden as she was by the wall which protected this property— were also coming to the beach most regularly. And the voices she could hear were *speaking* German! May lost no time in reporting this to the local FBI where she was not taken seriously and told politely but firmly to mind her own business and go home. Furious, but powerless, she did so. But the last laugh was hers. The voices she had heard belonged to the German servants of the estate next door. And yes, they were indeed preparing the landing of German submarines!

The situations May got into were not always of such a serious nature, for she loved life and parties and people and having fun. She was a good and loyal friend, certainly to me, over the years of our friendship. But woe to him who found himself on her private black list.

Her running feud with the Kennedy clan, almost from the day that Peter married Pat Kennedy, the sister of the then President of the United States, would fill a book. For much as she was forever faithful to those to whom she had opened her heart, so could she pursue the others with her wrath.

I'm sure that to her own family her many scrapes and the countless Cadillacs that she smashed up by driving them through the back door of her garage, must have been a source of great irritation. But to those like myself, who were not tied to her by blood relationships, all these extravaganzas were merely a source of laughter and added to her indomitably cheerful character.

I'm sorry to have to relate that her end was sad. A widow by then, in very reduced circumstances, and hardly helped in any way by Peter's in-law family, she was a very lonely little lady. Courageous yes, but lonely still. After Peter's engagement, the house on Sunset Boulevard was sold, since, as a married man, he intended to move away. After all the packing, crating and storing had been done, a friend came to pick up May in his car. It was the day of her final goodby to the house she had loved so much. When her friend drove up, May was standing there ready, a smart hat on her head. But under her arm she was carrying the number plate of the house she was leaving.

"For heaven's sakes, May," he said, "why are you taking this along?"

"Because," she replied, "I was so happy here, and who knows, perhaps I shall be lucky and find another house with that magic number, and be just as happy there all over again."

Franz Hohenlohe

(His Serene Highness Prince Franz Josef Antony zu Hohenlohe Waldenburg Schillingsurst of Vienna, Austria)

Foreword

By
Buddy Galon

Lady Lawford is a bitch. Indeed, a loving, caring, generous, intelligent, witty, and charming bitch; but, nevertheless a bitch. Webster's dictionary says that the term *bitch* may refer to a woman who is "malicious, spiteful, and domineering." What Webster's does not say is that in this case the *bitch* is also an attractive and talented internationally-recognized social and political personality. Years ago, Lady Lawford proudly said to me, "I have been called a bitch by the Aga Khan; by the Duke of Windsor; by Winston Churchill; by King Farouk; and by old Joe Kennedy. At least, I've been called a bitch by the best!"

It was a typically sunny California afternoon back in 1966, and I was the guest lecturer at the Symposium of Beverly Hills. After I had finished speaking, colorful Hollywood film personality Thelma Keaton flattered me so blatantly that I agreed to leave with her and go to meet an unnamed "sick friend". How was I to know that Thelma's "friend" would be Lady Lawford?

Lady May Lawford lay on a long coral-colored sofa surrounded by Oriental antiques, ivory and jade carvings and one entire wall of framed portraits. Dressed all in black and holding a black cat, she could have been on the current cover of *Town and Country* magazine— except for the incongruous presence of stark white bandages. "You can't kill the British with an axe!" was her defiant dismissal of her most recent mysterious brush with death. A long relationship with the most exciting and fascinating woman that I ever met began that day. Through the media I was familiar with Lady Lawford's son Peter— that he was an intimate of the Kennedy family, a close personal friend of Marilyn Monroe, and a member of Frank Sinatra's controversial inner-circle. However, it is sometimes over-looked that Peter's fame as an actor and as a friend to the famous can be traced back to the strong influence of his mother. Lady Lawford's love for the theatre was rabid, and her acceptance in international social circles was unquestioned.

From the very first day that we met, we both realized that there was a very special attraction between us. When we drove along the ocean near Carmel, California, our sparkling conversation turned to mysticism. In Mexico we vociferously debated international policies. Over tea at Lady Victoria Stevenson's, we politely discussed our mutual ancestor, Lady Arabella Churchill— the sister of the Duke of Marlborough, longtime mistress of King James II, and the mother of his four children including the Duke of Berwick. In Palm Springs, we gleefully "skinnydipped" after midnight. At a Santa Barbara dinner party, we giggled when the elderly German ambassador went to sleep and fell face-first into his French onion soup. These were truly wonderful times.

***

Now why would a royal-educated, world-traveled socialite-actress-political leader who married a knighted war hero and mothered a film actor who married into America's "First Family"— yes, why would she involve herself in a lasting relationship with a young All-American boy-next-door college student? (My friends point out to me that, despite my appearance, I can hardly be called a regular guy. They quickly remind me of my European studies for my doctorate degree; my sailing a prize-winning yacht; my successful career as a society entertainer; my Silver Cloud Rolls Royce; and my own group of aristocratic acquaintances and famous friends.) Yes, I suppose that does not make me a regular guy. However, would an extraordinary woman like Lady Lawford be happy with just an ordinary guy? Aware that many people commented on the differences in our ages, Lady Lawford and I simply ignored attempts by others to rob us of our happiness. We were both believers in reincarnation; thus accepting the fact that she arrived "too soon", or I arrived "too late" in this earthly existence.

On the occasion of her 1972 untimely and unnecessary demise, I eulogized Lady Lawford in newspapers from coast to coast. Paraphrasing my closing remarks, I stated that for several years I had enjoyed the pleasure of being her closest friend, her confidant, her intimate, her collaborator, and her escort. Besides her doctor, I was the last and only person with her at the time of her death. I loved her and respected her. Today I proudly acknowledge Lady Lawford's and my unannounced marriage that occurred on Easter Day, 1968.

Now, Lady May Lawford, as long as I have a voice to speak   or a pen   to write, your memory will live on.

Buddy Galon

Chapter One

Welcome To My Drawing Room

Ah, welcome to my drawing room. "Tisn't very nice, but it is home to me and the cats. No servants. No butler or French maid. Just me and the cats. Won't you sit down? Yes, there. That will be fine.

Or perhaps you'd prefer to sit over here on the sofa. Isn't it an atrocious monstrosity? I call its style Grand Rapids Modern. It is the only thing besides the television that is new in this room. That chair you are sitting in isn't really very comfortable— it is very old. Get up. Up! Get up, I said. Now lift the bottom of your chair. See, it is actually an old French— er— how do you say it?— a commode? I find it frightfully amusing, but awfully uncomfortable.

I have nothing in the house but some sherry. Would you care for a glass? Oh, if only I had a butler or a French maid to serve this correctly. I used to have some beautiful silver trays on which to serve, but they've been stolen. I had one beautiful silver tray that was a present from King George. It was inscribed: "George IV." Such a tray! It would be perfect for serving these biscuits. Here, try one. They are delicious. Mmmmmmmmm.

But what was I talking about? Oh, yes, silver trays. Once I had a very large and beautiful tray, quite heavy, which was handed down in my family from Queen Anne. I believe the Queen had presented it as a gift to one of her ladies-in-waiting as a reward for long and faithful service. Anyway, it was handed down in my family. So when my son Peter married Patricia Kennedy, I wanted to give them this priceless family heirloom. Just before the wedding, I took it to the jeweler's and had it engraved with their names on the back. I thought it was a lovely gift. Do you know what happened to that tray? A friend of mine saw it leaning against the wall on the dirty floor of Peter's beach house garage in Santa Monica. That brat and that bitch! Some way to treat a valuable heirloom! Honestly!

Some more sherry? It 'tisn't very expensive sherry. I think some monks or somebody squeeze it. No, I don't drink. Oh, maybe a glass of champagne now and then. Do you know what I really like the taste of? South— no, Southern Comfort. But just a small glass after dinner— like a liqueur, you know. I met the people who make Southern Comfort once at a party— the Fowlers up in Bel-Air. Nice people— yes, very nice.

Here, Poopsie, come to Mama. Here, I said, come up here on Mama's lap. Poopsie! Damned independent cat! But isn't she lovely? I just love animals. The striped one there— I call him Baby— was all alone in the world so I took him in. However, Poopsie is a black Burmese given to me by Herbert Hischemoeller— you know, the "Spice King," they call him. Anyway, they both live the life of Reilly. Livers and shrimps, shrimps and livers— that's all they'll eat. Spoiled rotten, they are. But God made animals and God made humans to take care of animals. I love all animals— especially horses, dogs and cats. That's why I always donate to the S.P.C.A. and the Pet Protection Association here in Los Angeles. Humans can take care of themselves, but I have always thought that we must care for the helpless animal. In London, I supported the Royal Society for the Prevention of Cruelty to Animals and even in North Africa I worked with a similar agency. Love animals and they will love you in return. Man! That's an altogether different matter.

Poopsie isn't the cat's real name. I just call her that for short. Of course, she is a female, but I had Captain Keagy, my veterinarian, neuter her. Now Poopsie and I have the same attitude toward sex as we do for oysters: We don't care for *either*.

Poopsie's real name is Queen Alexandra. I named her that because she has such an awful high-pitched, screechy voice. Meeeeee-owwwww! You see, when I was just a little girl— oh, maybe six— my mother introduced me to Queen Alexandra, wife of Edward VI. I curtsied politely and mumbled some pleasantry. Then the Queen spoke and never have I heard such an awful voice. It was worse than a peahen! And that's why I call my beautiful cat with the awful "meow" Queen Alexandra.

I've a darling story to tell you. There was a little boy and girl who questioned their father about how he met their mother. He said, "Oh, I met her in the garden— I helped remove a thorn from her paw." I love that! You know, women are such cats. My mother always told me to stay away from women; most are so unkind. Women never like me— I really can't understand why.

Those paintings? Oh, those are five-hundred-year-old Ming paintings. The four paintings which are on linen are extremely delicate because of their age. Don't you think they would be lovely in a museum?

And those— those are the Chinese Immortals— there are eight of them. Although they are deep-brown in color, they are of soap— or is it soapstone? Anyway, that's the Ho-Ho Bird there— it's my favorite. I've been told that they're a collector's item; personally I'm not mad about them.

Uh— yes— I suppose those flowers are pretty.

I've asked Miss Bonnie— that was my family name— she is Peter's secretary down at his Chrislaw Productions— I've asked her not to send me any more live flowers. I much prefer artificial ones— they don't have to be cared for, and they last ever so much longer. On Christmas or Easter, Milt Ebbins, Peter's manager, sends me out some flowers. Of course, I'm supposed to think they are from Peter, but I know Peter's handwriting— he uses long, bold strokes. So anyway, I call them up and gush my thanks for the damned live flowers that I don't like from that bastard son who won't even write a note much less visit me. Ah, but aren't these lovely silver vases— still they are such a pain to keep polished.

You will have another glass of sherry, won't you? As I said, I don't drink. Oh, like I said, an occasional glass of champagne— but my champagne drinking days are over. How the magnums flowed at one time, but where are those people who were always there when the champagne seemed never ending? Look at this newspaper clipping about my champagne days:

As usual, May Lawford had an internationally complexioned group on hand including, as it did, the George Bagnalls, well known sculptor Gladys Bush, Lady Elizabeth Carey, Mrs. Dodi Barnard (just returned from a world cruise) and Baron Charles de Grandcourt, the guest of honor's locally popular son. Also present were the Peter Hayes, June Allyson and Dick Powell, the Ross Vincents, beautiful Elizabeth Taylor, Baron and Baroness Vandermulen, Jim Schwatz, Princess Stephanie Hohenlohe, Fifi Ferry, Peter Lawford and Dr. Reuben L. McMaster.

Those were the General's medals there. Yes, I rather like that glass case with the blue velvet background. Look at all those medals! Sir Sidney was quite a leader. Sir Sidney— I always call him the General— has even more medals than these. That's the Queen's Medal... that one is St. Vladimir of Russia... there's St. Lazarus of Italy... Croix de Guerre of France and Belgium... oh, look at this one— it's the Legion of Honour. There are so many. I am leaving these to my grandson, Christopher, when I die. I hope that he will be proud of his grandfather's accomplishments.

Are you truly interested in these photographs on my drawing room wall? Oh, very well. That first portrait is of my grandfather, General Arthur Courtney Bunny of the Royal Artillery, who served forty-one years in India. Ugly old cuss, isn't he?

That portrait is of my father, Colonel Frederick W. Bunny, who also served in India. You know, my maiden name is French and should be pronounced "Bon-nay." I get so angry when people write it and pronounce my last name as if I were one of those Hugh Hefner Playboy rabbits!

Of course, you recognize the next portrait— my husband, Sir Sidney Barlow Turing Lawford of the Royal Fusiliers. My uncle and my brother— I come from an all Army family.

The General used to be very encouraging to me when I was a little blue. He used to say, "You know, May, you're not as ugly as you think you are." Wasn't that nice? He was so nice— so sort of— well, it's known as "patting you on the back." I had two very good-looking sisters— especially the sister that I told you about— the one with emphysema. Yes, Kathleen, who married a major in the Royal Army. She had been married to him for over a year and had been having sex with him all that time. She walked in front of the King's and Queen's doctor and so she said, "This s.o.b. says I'm still a virgin," and he said, "You are!" Figure that one out.

Their marriage was annulled and he gave her a thousand a year— I don't know what for. And off she went to Africa and on the way back she took up racing and she also took up with this Major— later the General— Dyer. He was a very tall man— six foot four— and a very, very fine cavalry officer. Kathleen and he were married and they went out to India. Her husband inherited from his mother and father— he was an only child— a big, huge estate in the middle of the forest; it used to belong to Robin Hood... wherever that is.

And Kathleen's husband leased Runnymead Epson where she could race these horses and every penny— until she died many years ago— she spent his money like a drunken sailor and her own money, too. She used to take these horses— two, four horses— four reins and train them. From India to Burma she would take them— the lot of them. Then they went back to Africa and they bought a farm in Kenya. She didn't like the farm as she got sick. Some man came to look at the farm and said he couldn't afford to buy it so she gave it to him. Gave it! They didn't sell it; they gave it to him. They returned to India and her husband became Chief of Staff under my husband, Sir Sydney.

My sister Gretta married a military man, too. She was such a beautiful rider and a beautiful shot and a concert pianist and terribly talented.

My sister Gretta, who was much younger and so much prettier than I, was married to General Glencairn Campbell. She had a son named Duncan Glencairn Campbell. He fell in love with the illegitimate child of Edward VII and Miss Willie James. Such a scandal— his mother was mortified. Later she married General Palmer and went to Rhodesia. After his death, she kept an apartment there, but felt so useless. She did not wish to marry; she said she didn't want anymore of that messy stuff insisting she was somewhere between "diapers and death." Without any training, she decided to become a secretary. By self-discipline, she taught herself typing and shorthand within three months. While working as a secretary, a long-time friend suggested that she join the Rhodesian Women's Army where she became alternately known to the service women as "the duchess" and "the bitchess."

I was the fool of the family— I did nothing! Yet we all married high-ranking officers in the British Army. It isn't strange. We were in the upper social class— which one shouldn't mention. It is the manner in which you are brought up. Who else would we meet?

We had nice manners and we knew how to behave like ladies. That was what the right sort of men were so particular about in those days. Men like the General, you see. Those men didn't look for very pretty chorus girls with beautiful legs and that sort of thing; they looked for a woman who would do them credit. They wanted a woman who they could take anywhere — to present to Her Majesty and take all over the Empire and say, "This is my wife." They wanted a wife that they knew would say the right thing, do the right thing and, if she entertained, she would do it impeccably. That's what they asked for; that's what they wanted. As my mother said, "Any man that you meet is a man who wants a wife who is a piece of white paper. The only person to write on it is him."

And in that frame is what we call a commendation. It reads:

Sir Jocelyn Lucas-Wright: I had the privilege of serving under Sir Sydney Lawford as his galloper from the time the Seventh Division left Alinsius 'till I was wounded and taken prisoner toward the end of the first battle. And later was his Aide-de-Camp in Cologne in the Crimson occupation. Two things will always remain in my mind. First, his personal courage and his regard for the welfare of his men. He picked himself up as the horse's head was galloping along and had taken a signaler's mount and rode on as if nothing had happened. A few days later, as every officer in the brigade had been killed or wounded, he led a successful charge against enemy trenches armed only with his cane. In the retreat, he stayed up all night fighting to get a train to save the wounded from further capture. He succeeded.

At Cologne, it was the same thing. He always thought of his men. Immaculate in appearance, jaunty in carriage, he was a great sportsman and a fine horseman. He will be remembered with affection and admiration by all who served under him.

In this picture, you can see why his men called the General "Swanky Syd." You see, he was always impeccable. That is old Seafoam standing next to the General in that picture. We called him Seafoam, but that was a slang word— because he liked a whisky bottle that comes like that, you know. But he isn't the one who sent the commendation to the General; Sir Jocelyn Lucas, who was his Aide-de-Camp the whole of the war, sent it, and no bigger damned fool ever lived because one day when they delivered to the Prince and his soldiers— the Prince had departed from there and left nothing but the Germans in front. That's when he got two horses shot from under him. When the Prince departed, Sir Sydney turned to Sir Jocelyn and said, "Jocelyn, take this letter to Page"— Page was Commander-in-Chief, who at that time was over him in command. And he said, "Take this to Page and tell him the British are gone. We are faced with nothing but four German divisions and there are but two of us. Don't worry; they are as good as dead." Some man— the General!

That is a photograph of DeGaulle there. He was quite young in that photo. I met DeGaulle at something in Paris— in fact, I met him several times. You know, I wasn't bad looking when I was quite young— seventeen or eighteen years of age.

And DeGaulle— he was just an ordinary officer then, I think he was a major— came along and seemed to be interested in me.

"I wonder if I can have a dance with you?" he asked.

"Thrilled to dance with you, love to dance with you," I'd say to DeGaulle; but while dancing, I'd have to say, "Do you mind if I have the use of lungs!"

That particular picture has a story.

Now one night about twelve o'clock, the telephone bell rang and it was some man who said,

"Is this Lady Lawford?"

"Yes," I said.

"I'd like so much to talk to your husband. This is Benito Mussolini."

"Go ahead, darling, talk to my husband." And then I added, "Musso, what do you want?"

"I'm in a heck of a jam because of—" and Mussolini went ahead to explain some military dilemma.

"Kick them in the back side!" I interjected.

"You don't understand. You don't know our fighting way," he said.

"Of course, but I know *our* fighting ways. You know we had the Twenty-Five Years War; we had the Hundred Years War; we had the Crimea; we had— oh, how many wars? You can't count them all."

Mussolini was the Wop of the whole of Italy. He was sort of the King of Italy. Or at least the real king was a damned fool so Musso took over as sort of King of Italy.

"What are you going to do?" I asked Sir Sydney after he had finished talking to Mussolini.

"I've got to take two regiments and go to Italy to see Musso. He's tangled up; he's no soldier," said Sir Sydney, who the following morning went off to Italy with his regiments.

I forget who he took or anything about it— I wasn't interested. So we heard afterwards that Sir Sydney— the General— made what he called "Lawford Sandwiches"— he had a line of battalions and a line of British and a line of battalions and a line of British. And when the General would say, "Now if I give the word *Fire,* the ones in front of you fire at his backside and you turn and fire at the other one's backside. You'll be dead anyway so you might as well go and fight!" Musso just gasped at this.

So Musso said to the General, knowing that Sir Sydney had a son named Peter,

"I'd like to get Peter something. I've nothing that Peter hasn't got so I'll send him my photograph."

So the General brought this photograph back in his kit and handed it to me and said,

"This is for Peter." Mussolini signed it— this is his handwriting— "For Peter Lawford" and his name. Later Peter brought the photograph to me and said, "Mother, it's a very beautiful horse and a very ugly man. Do you mind keeping it?"

You are quite sure that I'm not boring you? Here, have some more sherry.

Oh, that— that is a Christmas card signed "With our best wishes, Mary R and George R.I." That's the King and Queen of England— Mary Rex and R.I. for Regina, the Impress of India— to the Court of India. That was just the way they signed cards for friends. They were close friends of the General and so they sent him that Christmas card. I stuck the card there— I had nowhere to put it.

That is the King and Queen of the Belgians. The General was their greatest friend. That is why I hang their picture underneath his picture. And this card is from Elizabeth, the Queen of the Belgians, sent to the General. She sent him many, many of them. I think that there was a little— er. Lots and lots of letters came from her and she told us the truth about him. Her husband, the King of the Belgians, was killed by the Reds. Lots of people told me— the aides— you know, Daddy's age and people like that— said that Queen Elizabeth was always saying she liked him. She would like to go for a ride with him or she would like to do this and do that with him. Or couldn't they go to a party or a dance— all sorts of stuff. After all, my husband was a handsome man.

Is it seven-thirty? I mustn't miss the Perry Mason Show. I love Perry Mason. What's his name— Raymond Burr— or something. Such eyes! his is my very favorite television show, even the repeats. Do you think he might come to tea one day? Please invite him. Let's invite that nice Irish boy Dick O'Brien and Patrick Mahony and maybe Herbert Hischemoeller and "heels"— you know Miss Lane. And— click-clickety-clickety-click. That marvelous dancer that you know. How I enjoyed seeing her dance click-clickety-Eleanor Powell! Yes, that's her. Invite her to tea, too.

And that's Jack Kennedy. Jack is so different from all the people I used to know. He— he— I hate to say it because you're a Yank, you see, but— he was so *common*. You know, he used to turn 'round and say to his sister, "Aw, shuddup!" Yes, to Patricia he would say "Shuddup!"

Jack Kennedy— I can't forget his condition at the wedding dinner-dance. He said, "I heards you waz (hic) the best danzer around (hic). Why doncha dance with me?" I started to protest, not his drunken state, but his use of crutches as a result of a skiing accident, I believe. Just then he threw down his crutches and whirled me around the floor. The photographer snapped us. Jack almost fell. He was such a likeable fellow— that Jack. I think I like him the best of the Kennedys.

This picture of Nehru— years ago when I was very young, I met him. I don't remember any incidents about him, but he was supposed to be very up-and-coming. I don't think he liked Ghandi. I called him a naked savage— he was! He just had a *dotee*— what the Indians call a loin cloth. Few people know that Ghandi had considerable wealth despite his vow or oath of poverty— he owned several salt mines.

That picture is the Duke of Windsor when he was quite young— yes, 1922. That is before the General ordered him off his horse. You see, he was playing polo and Lady McCavin, wife of the Governor, came up to me and said,
"My God, that boy's going to break his neck!"
"Well," I said, "I'll go speak to Sir Sydney about it." So I went and fetched him, saying, "Is there anything you can do to get that boy off that horse before Lady McCavin has chickens? She's just scared stiff!"
The Duke of Windsor has drunk since the age of nine. He drank a bottle of whiskey from nine o'clock in the morning until twelve. At twelve, he would rest up and then get another one. He was an alcoholic of the worst kind— incorrigible.
So seeing him drunkenly playing polo, I said,
"Sydney, you've got to do something."
"Yes, yes," the General replied, "he's going to break his neck anyway."
"Yes, but I don't want him to do it here at the cocktail party."
"Sydney," I repeated, "you have got to do something. Get him off that horse."
"I don't know what I can do. How will I get him off the horse when he will not get off?" the General continued.

"Pull rank on him, for Christ's sakes!" I retorted.

At that time, Sir Sydney was of higher military rank than the Duke, who eventually was to become King of England. The Duke protested when my husband tried to coax him off the horse. "I wanna die, I wanna die. and I'm not getting off this horse," he whined. However, when the General ordered him to dismount, the Duke did so sullenly.

That picture is me addressing the United Empire Party at Caxton Hall. It was a very conservative group of mostly socially-prominent people— however, there were some peasants. Lord Beaverbrook was the head along with Lord Rothemire. I was the chairman.

Once while I was speaking at Caxton, a lady who was sitting on the left front row heckled me. Her bedraggled appearance and Irish brogue tagged her a peasant.

"How come the chairman of the British United Empire Party is wearing a Paris hat?" she asked me.

I snapped back, "Because such a goose as you can't make them as good!"

I was looked up to and admired by thousands of people. The House of Parliament recognized and respected me. One day, Peter's tutor asked to have a word with me.

"Your ladyship, I realized that you are very pleased with your successful political endeavors, that you enjoy the adulation of the public and that your ego is well-fed by this career; but what about the General? He never sees you in the mornings, you occasionally lunch with him, and in the evenings, you see him mainly at dinners and parties attended by large numbers. Most of his time he spends blowing dust off of his dry martinis at his club. Although he isn't young, he still is quite youthful to have headed four squadrons in World War One. Now he deserves some pleasure in life— his single pleasure being travels. He loves to travel. But he likes companionship— *your* companionship. Yet you are much too busy with your new career to see him or to travel."

That evening, I told the General to go ahead with the trip to the Bahamas he had mentioned before, but he would not hear of leaving Peter and me. I then said that he wouldn't have to leave me. Lord Beaverbrook did not want to accept my resignation, exclaiming that they could never find another like me. I always said exactly what I thought, regardless. But that was the end of the political career of Lady May Lawford.

That was the Aga Khan there; he was one of my greatest friends. I used to meet him all over. The First War, I met him in India. And I'll tell you about his harem.

Aga married. You see, when they married, they were about fourteen or fifteen. Of course he married a native wife— to begin with. And she was in the harem, but she never came out unless she was driving around in carriages with shutters. You know these shutters that you pull? Sometimes they're on windows. She could look out the shutters, but could never be seen.

I was talking to the Aga Khan— there were a couple of grooms behind— and I switched from talking Hindustani to English and French. And he said to me,

"I wish you— you talk such wonderful Hindustani— I wish you'd go and see my wives."

"God Almighty," I said. "How many have you got? It's a wonder you can ride a horse even!"

"Really, May," he said, "you are the most amusing girl I ever met in my life."

"Well, when do you want me to go to see them?" I asked.

"Any time you pass my house," he answered, referring to his lovely palace— a great, big white palace, "you go in and see my wives."

One day I was out exercising a mare— I expected to sell her for— ah— about 1600, and I was taking her walking past his palace. My God, I thought, I need a drink. You know the kind of drink I mean— either water or lemonade or something. I was riding astride; I either rode astride or the other way— it didn't make any difference to me. So I went up and banged on the door and I said that the Aga had said, "You can come call on me and the wives." There were about eight of them. Eight! I once asked him, "How in the hell do you make a selection? You really must say, 'Eeny, meeny, miny, mo' by counting them by the toe."

I went in— you never saw such a room— about fifty times the size of this. And it had in every corner of it these great big colored balls that you put on Christmas trees. You know what I mean? Oh, about *that* size. And it had a music box in *that* corner and a music box in *that* corner and *that* and *that* and they were all playing at once— different tunes. It wasn't Christmas; this was just every day.

So then they came and talked to me and I was dressed in a riding habit—britches and long brown boots up to here, and white gloves and an ascot tie— a neckerchief. They— the wives— asked me all sorts of questions in Hindustani.

"What have you done that your husband doesn't love you?"

"I don't know what you're talking about."

"You have no jewelry."— I had a wedding ring and a watch on— that was it.

"He must not love you."

"How do you know he doesn't?"

"Well,"she said, "because he lets you out, and other men look at you."

"So what?"

"I've seen," one stated, "where some women are allowed to dance in public."

"Sure, I danced with the Aga's nephew, Jete, and with a lot of people."

They gasped. They thought it was awful. Their only public appearance was when the carriage would come around. They would get in the carriages and they would all sit like that. The shutters were pulled down so there was no air. No air— it must be stifling!

The Aga Khan's nephew was a great friend of mine. Didn't I tell you that the Aga left his prince— one of his princes— with me? No, not his son Aly— he was much older. This was his young nephew— Jete. Jete was the son of a colored— a black woman. I sold Jete one of my horses and I also helped him learn to speak the King's English.

When the Aga Khan became a certain age, he was in Monte Carlo. His wife— the Begum— was in Monte Carlo, too. She was the daughter of the man who owned a tremendous lot of hotels in a certain province of India. Which province it was I can't remember.

We had them to lunch at Ravelagh. Daddy was one of the first member of the Ravelagh Club in London. It was a tremendous occasion with a receiving line. At least four-hundred people shook hands with us— and with me. And I said to the General, "For God's sake, do something about it. My hand is sore!" So he ended the ritual and we had lunch— the four of us. The Begum couldn't speak a word of English, but she spoke beautiful French.

The Aga had more race horses than anyone in the world. You knew that, didn't you? And his horses were running in the Derby that we all attended. Ten of his horses won the Derby— the whole Derby! He said to me.

"Are you betting on anything in the next Derby?"

I replied, "Yes, what about you?"

"Oh," he said, "I never bet; I never put a nickel on anything."

However, the Aga and the Begum went away— I forgot where they went to— Scotland, I think, to stay with Lord Somebody or Other. Anyway, on their very first night back in Monte Carlo, the Begum said to me,

"May, darling, how wonderful to see you." She said this in perfect English.

I said,"How on earth did you learn to speak English?"

"I listened to Jete. He taught me English; he talked to me in English all the time.'

So there my English lessons to young Jete had led to the Begum learning English, too.

When the Aga died, the Begum came here to America. We had a house on Sunset Boulevard and she came over there. We had a big party for her. Oh, she was very pretty. And when she went away, she said to me, "I'm going to send you my picture" and she sent me this.

Oh, dear, do you have to leave now? I wish that you did not have to go. The cats and I have enjoyed your visit so much. But I'm afraid that I have bored you stiff. There's just nothing as frightfully boring as an old relic living in the past. Most people today aren't interested in an old bag like me recounting boring stories about my past, but you *did* seem interested.

Can you come again soon? Perhaps you would be my guest for dinner one evening next week? Oh, no, I won't try to cook— even the cats dislike my cooking. I have not tried to cook since the General and I were living at the Everglades Club in Palm Beach in 1940. We had come in from the theatre and, it being the cook's night off, I thought

I would prepare us a light snack. I was never allowed in the kitchen as a child, but a baked potato seemed an easy choice to prepare. After washing the potatoes and putting on the oven after placing the potatoes inside, I noticed that the pilot light was not burning. Many minutes elapsed while the General and I searched for a match. What a sound when at last I struck the match to the gas-filled oven! My eyebrows and the front hair on my head did not escape the fire, not to mention my burned face and hands. On paying my medical bills and bringing me home from the hospital, the General made me promise never to try to cook again. He insisted those baked potatoes were the most expensive cuisine for which he had ever footed the bill!

Anyway, I know a nice place to dine in Century City that has quite edible vegetables. We could go there if you like. And won't you please take my telephone number so that you may call me soon? I'd like that. Oh, here's a clipping from the newspaper that might interest you; I found it most interesting. No need to return it. Take it with you.

Thank you for a very nice afternoon. Goodbye. Watch your step on those stairs. Goodbye.

Chapter Two

Lady Lawford: Beginning Of A Bitch

When I was four-years-old, the family cat disappeared, and along with it so did I. The family did not miss the cat, but they did miss me. For nearly fourteen hours, they searched for me. Finally I came wearily walking in to the amazement of my family and I exclaimed, "That bloody cat ran away!" as my explanation. They were all aghast at my use of the curse word "bloody" at only four-years-old.

Oh, such a story! Are you shocked at me? My father used to say only a tart or a duchess can use the word "bloody" properly. But only a duchess can say the word without it sounding vulgar. I remember the old Duchess of Gloucester used the word profusely and with dignity when on a hunt. And old Lady Something Lawford used it well.

We were reared to be very strong. My mother came in from horseback riding with both collar bones broken. My sister rushed to assist her off the horse. My mother said, "Pshaw, what are collar bones for if not to break?" Once I was thrown by my horse on a high jump— I was only about five— my mother slapped me across the rear, chided my tears and placed me on the horse again to make the same jump. When my sister climbed on a sofa and screamed at seeing a rat, my mother scolded her greatly. My brother Bryce was treated very sternly as a child. Later he was shot through both arms during the English battle with India, and he remained shell-shocked for eighteen months before dying. Never once did we go to see him. Of his death, my mother said, "He gave his life for his country. Is there a better death?"

Once, when we were living in Ceylon, and I was only seven or eight-years-old, my sister and I were in the care of two lovely young Ceylonese governesses. What a beautiful cinnamon garden there was! It was at least forty acres of wonderfully-scented blossoms among which there were religious statues and a particularly lovely Buddhist temple. Of course, both of our governesses were devout Buddhists. I noticed one day as the priest was reading the service, his eyes kept wandering over to my governess— undoubtedly, he found her amusing to look at— I mean, pretty. On one later occasion, as she was walking me through the gardens, he offered to show her the tooth of Buddha which was supposed to be inside the small brown temple encased in a golden casket and locked with a gold key. My governess was eager to accept his offer, but I said, "No, she can't leave me." He said to me, "Well, what are your terms?" Even at that tender age, I was a rather conniving, mercenary bitch! So I stated that I, too, wanted to see the tooth. "Oh, but you are not a Buddhist." "Then *she* can't leave me to see it with you. I'll tell my father if she does," I threatened. "You can see it another day," he said as he led my governess up inside the empty temple. She returned some forty-five minutes later. Can you imagine? I bet she was a tart! My mother hired a young tart as my governess!

I received my education at Princess Helena's School. Princess Helena was Queen Victoria's eldest daughter, who was still alive and running the exclusive finishing school. One day I remember a great hush over the school. I asked why, but got no answer. I was perhaps twelve or thirteen at the time. Even my sister would not explain and certainly not my mother.

It was not until I was married that I learned the whole story behind the big hush. It seems that the exclusive girls' school shared athletic courses with a boys' school. Several of these boys, after an athletic event, forced themselves into a girls' dormitory. They had already known the girls they came to visit. Of course, the boys were armed with all kinds of delicacies and liquors. It must have been quite an evening because three or four of the girls— generals' daughters— had to leave for Paris where their babies were cut out. That is murder!

For years and years I never understood a joke or repartee I once heard. One day, what a lovely top hat and veil I was wearing! Anyway, there was a plump kitchen cook with her fat hands clasped under her long white apron and excitedly watching the hunt. The man who was my escort pulled a very difficult maneuver and fell backward. The old lady asked him smilingly, "How many times are you on you back?"

"Not as many times as you, I bet," he retorted.

Upon hearing this talk, I asked him, "You mean she rides the hounds?"

He just laughed at me and my not understanding.

"You're a weird one— yes, you are."

When I was about sixteen, my mother took me to the matinee at the Prince of Wales Theatre in London. The program fare was *The Degenerates* starring Mrs. Lily Langtry. Oh, she was divine— such a tiny waist— oh, what a figure! And hair— kind of honey colored— I am sure it was not her own color. She charmed me completely. When we left the theatre, I was walking on air and I knew I wanted to be just like Lily Langtry. To which my mother merely replied:

"Oh, pshaw! Forget such absurd notions."

That evening, after dinner, when my father asked me— according to protocol— a child only speaks when spoken to.

"What happened to you today, May, anything interesting?"

Immediately I began to tell of the afternoon at the theatre much to my mother's dismay. She was fervently trying to prevent my telling him of seeing *The Degenerates* and of my burning desire to become an actress. My mother took her handkerchief and wiped her eyes and asked to leave the room. My father said a stern "no," saying he wanted to talk to her. But first, he told me to go to my room and memorize all the verses in the Bible about Jezebel, and to come back down at ten and quote them. The butler looked at me as I went out the door and said, "Blimey, Miss May, you've done tore it this time!"

At ten, I returned and quoted the Scriptures and my father lectured on the fact that there are no good women in the theatre.

Yet I always admired Lily Langtry. Although she was married to Mr. Langtry, who often attended the house parties of King Edward, it was a well-known fact that for years she was the King's mistress— and evidently with her husband's permission!

Her father was the Dean of Jersey, a high position on the island. Many times I remember my mother visited them there. Because they were distantly related to the Queen, Lily had her debut at Buckingham Palace with full honors. My parents were in attendance. But later, after she saw Ellen Terry and decided to become an actress, she lost her social acceptance in the court circle. Her years as the mistress of King Edward caused her to fall even farther from social circles.

One day, my father saw her and the King— yes, he was the grandfather to the Duke of Windsor— walking down Bond Street. They were stopped in front of Cartier's— before it moved from Bond Street— where she was admiring a wide diamond bracelet. The King was saying, "Why, I've spent enough *on* you to build a battleship!"

To which she quickly retorted, "And you've spent enough *in* me to sink that battleship."

My father quoted this story, but I did not understand it until after my marriage. My husband explained it to me.

My sisters were presented at court to the Queen as was my mother. In fact, my mother went through the same presentation in Ireland— it is really quite expensive. The time came for me to be presented. At the same time, I was madly in love with a beautiful horse. Oh, I wanted that horse more than anything in the world. Yes, even more than being presented to the court circle! So my father gave me a choice and I chose the horse. I've never been sorry.

When I was eighteen, my father decided I must do something— either become a nurse in Princess Alexander's nurse service (ugh!) or a governess. After all, I was well-educated; I spoke three languages— German then, but not now. One other choice was to become a teacher in the Princess Helena school. Or marry!

When I was suffering from the theatre bug, my mother had begun to search around for a suitable husband for me to take my mind from such "foolish ideas."

My father suggested the very wealthy old Lord Berry since "you aren't very sexy." He had a magnificent estate with many millions, but he was in a wheelchair. I never cared much for him and, eventually, he fell from his wheelchair and died.

My second choice for a mate was a fine doctor on Harley Street. He too was much older and quite well-to-do. He told me I was pretty— nobody else ever did. We had a fine wedding with white horses, white feathers in my hair and a mile-long train.

After the wedding, he asked me, "What do you want to do tonight?"

"Go dancing," I said.

"No," said he. "You must be quite tired. Why don't you go up and get undressed?"

He then came up and kissed me *on the lips*— the first time ever for me! Then he started some other shenanigans. I leaped from the bed crying. The whole night I, in my nightdress, sat downstairs sobbing unceasingly and hysterically. My groom walked downstairs somewhat disgruntled and placed the Bible next to me. It was opened to the passage that started, "Wives, submit yourselves unto your mates, and so on."

The next morning, I went home. My mother and father tried to explain to me that such was a natural part of marriage. My aunt, who was visiting us also tried to talk to me. And all were quite upset with me.

That afternoon, as well as that morning, our doctor tried further to help me face my personal dilemma. Reluctantly, I returned to my groom and he promised to help me learn the art of love.

It was so messy. It was the only part of marriage that I could not stand.

Very shortly my new husband left his private practice and joined the Royal Army. There he was an Army surgeon soon to become Colonel. So off to India we went.

When my first husband and I were en route to India just after our marriage, we were staying in our compartment to eat dinner one evening. A dark-skinned hand reached through the curtains from the next berth. I took my fork and pinned the hand by the palm to the solid surface. While I went around to the other compartment, after getting an attendant, the hand worked itself loose and was nowhere to be seen. My bridegroom admonished me for my behavior; he was not pleased at my action.

Each evening at dinner, I remained very reserved and quiet, no sparkle or gust of energy to appear in high enough spirits for a bedroom display. But I always did think I looked my best when I wore a lovely chiffon nightdress— usually blue— and a dainty nightcap.

My husband used jewels from Cartier's and a most beautiful horse to tempt me. He was very kind about it. First he'd knock on my door, then he'd bring in a lovely bracelet or brooch.

I was expected to exchange my favors for these trinkets. Honestly, I felt like a tart— yes, a French tart! Finally in disgust, my husband would exclaim,

"I'd rather be in bed with a dead policeman! You're like sleeping with a wet umbrella! You become so stiff and cold. All you can say is two phrases— *don't* and *hurry up*. It's a good thing you don't have to make your living off of sex; you'd starve to death."

My first husband, Tubby— he was a bit chubby— that's why I called him Tubby. However, he had a very fine last name. It was Vaughn-Aylen. Sixty thousand dollars he had paid for his practice on Harley Street. You know he was to become the head dermatologist of all India? That's why I have such a good complexion.

Tubby taught me to be basically vegetarian— not to eat meats. He said that when the cattle are just about to be slaughtered, they realize it. The anticipation of death causes an increase of adrenaline in their system. This adrenaline can be harmful when consumed by humans. Not so with fish or fowl or so Tubby said. Look how rosy my cheeks are and here— feel my smooth skin. I do owe my good complexion to my first husband.

We got on amazingly well, except for one thing— you guessed it. He kept giving me horses, diamond bracelets and other animals— dogs and cats— in exchange for my— my— oh, balls! My *body*. I used to ask him what he found so amusing about my body. I found all of that so dirty. I used to grit my teeth and clench my hands while he mauled me over. Even with his just-bathed skin, his lovely eau-de-cologne and his beautiful silk pajamas, I still felt him and *both* were so dirty. He really hurt my feelings by telling me how bad I was in bed. He told me that when they would give the girls in the call-house champagne, I wouldn't even get a crust of bread! Imagine that! And him sleeping with every black nigger in India!

You know, I once had an experience with a lesbian. In the north of India were the three great races like the Gold Cup, Calcutta Cup and Navy Cup. Since I lived about seven miles out of town, I wished to go into town to stay during the races. Of course, my husband was away during the races. Arriving in my own buggy, I checked into a major hotel. During some of the festivities, I was introduced to the Ambassador from Turkey and his wife. My, he was a tall, dark and handsome man, while she was quite petite and dainty. She immediately felt my dress and complimented me on it. Too, she touched my long hair— I had dark hair before I became red-haired— and commented on its luster. Her husband was called back on official business, but she planned to go on with her ball. She, of course, invited me. And by some coincidence, we were in adjoining rooms in the hotel. After the ball, I said good night to her at my door and I went in to go to bed. Only a few moments passed when she appeared at our adjoining door, *stark naked.* She then rushed toward me, telling me how beautiful I was and how much she wanted to hug and kiss me.

"I have never loved my husband and I cannot bear to have sex with him," she cried.

Amazed, I abruptly pushed her away and warned her not to touch me. After all, I studied boxing with the former middleweight champion. Poor soul. I never saw her again.

I would not be at all surprised if Thelma Keaton isn't a lesbian. She is always fawning over me. She once said to me, "Do you love me, do you love me?"

To which I retorted, "Balls! What do you think I am— a lesbian?"

Such a strange woman— she is always saying that we have so much in common since "we are both actresses." I don't consider myself an actress. And I secretly laugh at the way Thelma Keaton introduces me to her *friends?* She always says, "This is my wonderful and dear friend *Lady* Lawford!" Where does she get such breeding? I am sure she wouldn't bother with me at all if I had no "handle."

Once I remember our chauffeur in India served me with his notice to leave our employ. I offered him more money— he was a good servant— but he said that did not matter.

"What then is the cause?" I asked him.

He replied, "I am freezing to death every night waiting on your husband."

You see, we had an understood agreement that I could go out with others dancing, while my husband would find his amusement at some lady's apartment or house. The poor chauffeur had to sit outside and wait in the bitter cold for the doctor to return until four o'clock in the morning sometimes. He remained after I gave him more money, two wool blankets and always a thermos of hot coffee. Of course, I threatened to kill him if he ever divulged any of the activities of my husband... and he never did!

After only a short time in India, I became quite sick with malaria. The one redeeming fact of the disease was that I did not have to sleep with my husband.

In the meantime, the chauffeur told me that my husband was seeing another woman. "Good!" I thought down underneath. My malaria fever continued so at last my husband came to me with two tablets to relieve my high temperature. While my husband was out to get me water with which to take the pills, the butler, who was standing nearby, quickly took the tablets from me and substituted aspirin. This was my first brush with what could have been death. The tablets turned out to be oleander— a drug that can cause insanity.

After eighteen months, I could take no more. I first went to Bombay. While in Bombay— the doctor had prescribed a ten-day rest there— my husband opened my door at the King Edward Hotel just across from the "Taz" (Mahal). He had discovered I was leaving him by checking my ticket to London and shouting, "If I can't have you, no one else shall!" He then tried to push me out the second-story window. I kicked him in the you-know-where and fled.

Since he was up for a high hospital appointment in Southampton, he didn't want the publicity of an attempted murder charge. We had lived for quite some time under an arrangement: I would be his wife and maintain the household and servants; his sex he was to find elsewhere. Much later, he and Daddy reached an agreement by which our marriage was annulled.

I remember Captain Berthanhy-Leslie whom I met at Hong Kong— can you imagine Thelma Keaton vacationing in Jackson Hole, Wyoming, instead of some place like Hong Kong? He had inherited half of Scotland— what's that lovely song they wrote about one of his estates? La-la-la-la. It was after my first marriage; this was nearly five years since I lived with him. Since my mother did not approve of divorce, my husband and I had an understanding about our marriage by which we would live apart. Anyway, I arrived in Hong Kong where I was met by my mother and father. On that evening, some Italian royalty was having a dinner-dance, and he requested my presence if I could attend on such short notice. The table was arranged according to rank— generals, lords, colonels, majors, captains and so on down. Beside me was this Berthanhy-Leslie— there was a famous doctor with the name Berthanhy. Our conversation turned to opium and I was greatly interested in the subject. He offered to take me to an opium den. Oh, such an experience, I shall never forget. What a smell! What trance-like appearances the people had. To get to the den, we had to go down many, many steps to a deep, dark cellar. There lay on a bed of reeds one man who was in a trance from opium and had been for fifteen days. They said he hardly ate. When I asked about his body eliminations, they said that he just continued to lie there. Occasionally they would lift his legs to wash and disinfect him.

Daddy wanted me to marry "Billy" very much; he much approved of the match. The Captain even gave me a ring, but I returned it when he told me he wanted *nine* children. He planned to leave each of his proposed nine children one of his large estates. No thanks! I wrote him later from London, returning his ring and declining his proposal of marriage. One day, my father announced, "Billy is in London."

I saw him at lunch the next day, but never again. *Nine* children. What a wonderful dancer he was! And I'm sure he had no problem with his money finding a wife to have his nine offsprings. You know, I was never attracted to money. Even Lord Berry— major, he was in the Royal Army— you know, he had been kicked by a horse down there. Oh, what a magnificent estate he had outside London! No, even his money could not sway me. What would I do with a man in a wheelchair? Oh, but he could never dance and I do love to dance. The men I like best for dancing are Russians— they are divine dancers. Then Americans and finally the English. The man offered my father one hundred thousand pounds for my hand in marriage. Oh, but children— *nine* children!

... On to my father's house in London. My mother had died at Malta while I was away. Later my husband died, leaving everything to his girlfriend. I got nothing! Not even my fifty evening dresses or my beautiful horse. No, I didn't go to his funeral.

Now I was a young widow, captured by my doting father, who would not let me go out unescorted at all. I was virtually held a captive in my father's prison— his house.

Oh, how I abhor the color green. Even when Daddy sent me a Rolls Royce out to our place for my birthday, I couldn't stand it— it was *green*. But I told Daddy that it was too hard to drive and I wanted a motor car that did not demand a chauffeur.

One day when I was driving around Los Angeles, I was next to an accident, so I pulled to the side and got out. A huge Rolls Royce had smashed into one of those Hitler cars— those fragile Volkswagen things. The Volkswagen driver was visibly upset over his nearly-demolished auto. However, the Rolls Royce owner said, "Well it's your fault."

"What do you mean— my own fault?" the little Jew asked.

The other driver snapped back: "It wouldn't be so bad if you didn't drive a piss-pot!"

Remember, I had never been kissed on the lips until my wedding day. Even in my second marriage, there was little passion. The General— Sir Sydney Lawford, an old friend of my father— proposed to me when we were out looking at Lady What's Her Name's beautiful estate. There was a lovely small chapel which we went into. The General was not himself that day. He was very quiet and depressed. When I asked him what was his trouble, he explained that he must return to head the Chestnut Division in India, his large house and his four beautiful horses in about a month. Then he looked at me seriously and asked, "Will you go with me?"

I suppose it was the horses that did it— I loved horses. It was just the getting away from my father's tyrannical orders, too. He never treated me as a woman who had been married and used to freedom. I could not even read in my bedroom after ten o'clock!

That evening, after dinner and long conversations— it was the General's sister's estate— Lady Evanston. I remember now because there was a blood stain on the drawing room floor just at the base of the staircase which could never be removed. Every time they thought that they were rid of the stain, it would return. Anyway, we both walked up those stairs to our respective bedrooms— they were side by side. When I said good night and opened the door to my bedroom, he followed me in my door.

I froze! My lips trembled and my fingers turned to ice. The General was kind and gentle, but I thought to myself, "Oh, no, not this again!"

The General and I were married in a quiet civil ceremony at Caxton Hall in London. However, I think our marriage records were destroyed during the war when a blitz would hit every five minutes.

Peter was an awful accident! I did everything to prevent such an accident... including the cause of such accidents. After I married, I used to lie awake and make up excuses to my husband to keep from having to endure that horrible, messy, unsanitary thing that all husbands expect from their wives. If only the Bible had not said, "Wives, submit yourselves unto your husbands."

I can still remember slipping to the kitchen and getting uncooked meat which I rubbed against my nightdress. I was *always* having my period! But, oh, that horrible time when I really did not have my period. I rushed to Lord Evans to hear my fears confirmed— I was two-and-a-half months pregnant. Oh, God! Even too late for an abortion— of course, I don't believe in that anyway— it's murder. I've never approved of abortion. Yet I never wanted Peter.

I had some lovely maternity dresses and gowns made and it really wasn't so bad. The General wasn't even near when it came time for me to deliver. I shall never forget it— such agony! I still remember having a revolver under my pillow. When the labor pains became so intense, I took the gun and placed its barrel to my mouth. At that moment, the nurse came in and kept me from pulling the trigger. That's how bad the pain was. The doctor who attended Peter's birth was of the same name as an attendant in the wedding of Princess Margaret.

I can't stand babies! They run at both ends; they smell of sour milk and urine. I never saw Peter until he was washed and perfumed. Ugh! Peter was such a mistake! No, I don't think Peter knows he was an accident. It might hurt him if he knew. But I made the General promise that there would be no more babies— *ever!*

Chapter Three

Peter Lawford:
Beginning Of A Bastard

Oh, thank goodness for little things. The General was old, and did not bother me much. In fact, I never had sex with him after Peter was three. My first husband was the one who really bothered me; it was he who led me to a nervous breakdown. I also blame my mother and father. They should have prepared me for what was to happen. I knew babies didn't come by stork, but I didn't really know exactly how. I just assumed God sent them somehow.

My first husband was good-looking to me, clever, and quite bright or he wouldn't have been in Harley Street. But he immensely enjoyed amusing himself with that unsanitary, disgusting sex habit. Probably we could have done well had it not been for that. After all, he loved the manner in which I managed the servants and attended to all the household duties. As a horsewoman and hostess, I was superb, but as for the other— oh, forget it!

I've been reading a book called *Valley of the Dolls* that I found out by the garbage. It has been years since I've read a book other than a mystery or suspense novel. This book— I've never read such! Many things I must read over and over. The girl in it has a strange word with which she refers to her breasts. "Boobs" or something like that. I've never heard of it. And the little rubber hats the men use as contraceptives. What an extraordinary idea! To think that I am learning about such things at this late age. And the girl gives the little rubber hats to the fellow. I wonder if either of my husbands ever used such things with me? I certainly never knew it. However, I should know— I often submitted myself as often as once a month. One time I remember twice a month! But in this book, it occurs much more often. I am luckier than I thought. Thank goodness, my husbands were older and didn't request all that messy act more than once a month!

Here on another page, it tells exactly how I felt about it all: "He felt her response was that of a lady and he, being a gentleman, respected it." I always thought that it was something for a woman to endure and a man to enjoy. Never did I think that if the male were not so "unsophisticated" in his behavior that a female might derive some pleasure. If perhaps the man had treated me gently and held me close and offered genuine affection, I, too, might have enjoyed the act. I really have desired a closeness with someone. But neither of my husbands had kissed me on my mouth until the wedding ceremonies and I trembled like everything. I must admit I didn't enjoy it when at last my first husband did kiss me there.

Once, after I was married, I was looking at some horses with a gentleman. Growing quite tired later in the day, I lay down under a tree to catch a moment of sleep. I awakened to a soft, gentle kiss quietly planted on my lips. I don't even remember the gentleman's name, but I remember liking the kiss. I had terrible guilt feelings and prayed to God for forgiveness for a long, long time.

When Peter was quite young, I procured the Baroness Purceval's— the baroness' father painted all those lovely works— governess for his upbringing. She spoke five languages fluently and was quite strict. One day, she came to me and asked for her severance pay; she was leaving. I demanded an explanation. She exclaimed, "I will not govern Peter if you continue to allow him to associate with such!"

She was referring to Prince Rainier, who was about the same age as Peter. It seems that the prince's father had a laundress who neatly arranged all of his shirts after washing and ironing them. One day, he raped her— this proved to be a great moment in the life of the laundress. She went to the priest and told him what had happened. She even offered to send him to Rome to have the Pope pardon her. Whether she became pregnant from the prince's father— a Grimaldi— or another boyfriend was never quite decided. Anyway, Prince Rainier arrived shortly after her marriage to the prince's father.

When at last a wife was to be found for this "child of rape," no suitable member of royalty would consent. Then he met John Kelly's daughter who had by now become a Hollywood star. I knew old Kelly. He was just a common Irish builder. He built the nigger shanties that adjoin the golf course. He was a nice fellow, and I often invited him to our parties. Then there was his family which moved to Philadelphia. Grace was a lovely, lovely girl. They had a dream for her— make her a queen, princess or something. The idea of considering Prince Philip marriage material for her! Anyway, Grace stands out because forty thousand dollars was paid to keep her off of the casting couch. What a wedding they did have! The Kelly dream was fully realized. Of course, the royal families of Europe, for the most part, ignored the affair. I certainly add Rainier to the level of that whore, the Duchess of Windsor, and that photographer, Antony Whatshisname.

Like many European children, Peter led a highly supervised life. I personally, carefully selected his nurses, governesses and tutors; interviewed and "weeded out" those whose manners, voice and diction did not come up to my standard and who might have been lax in failing to correct the small courtesies that are the hallmark of a cultured gentleman— such as licking his fingers when playing cards or reading a magazine; keeping his hat on in the elevator; going through a door before a woman— any woman! —; eating between meals; and breaking into a conversation.

I set his daily lessons which commenced at nine in the morning and finished at one o'clock. After his breakfast at eight, he came to my room for family prayer— an old English tradition. After lessons, he would come for a walk with me and we would lunch together at home or in a restaurant.

Always we said "spend a penny" as our statement signifying a desire to go to the bathroom.

The thing I was most strict about was good manners, and I lost a nice young governess because she made Peter enter the car in front of her. Young Peter had fifty lines to write which read "Ladies First." Interrupting the conversation was another rock on which we split. On my return home at his bed time, if his governess or tutor reported he had been "difficult" or "disobedient," I would discuss the matter with both— separately, of course— and if discipline was necessary, then Peter was deprived of something he liked— like tennis or the Gala dinner and floor show— a real punishment! Had he committed some vulgarity or breach of good manners, then bed for several hours after his lunch the next day.

His food was of the simplest— the formula given me by two famous doctors, now dead. Anything he disliked was not on his menu. Meat three times weekly; plenty of vegetables, fruits, one hundred percent whole wheat bread, sweet butter, brown sugar or honey. No canned food of any kind. No pastries and only plain cake and hard cake after lunch and dinner. Milk twice a day, fruit juices, white wine and water he drank at lunch and dinner. No snacks between meals!

After lunch he would lie down with a book for an hour— perhaps more. Then his governess or tutor would take him for tennis or ballet lessons for grace and deportment, swimming in the sea, visiting ships of all nations in the harbor, an afternoon cinema— if raining— or entertaining his little friends at home or going to their houses.

He dined at eight; was in bed by nine and— when in Monte Carlo— once weekly accompanied us to the Gala at the Casino to see the floor show.

In the beginning he had no homework. When he was older, he had Spanish, German and music added to his studies. He read only selected books— English fairy stories, English and French classics; no crime stories. Having studied Peter so long, I decided he was quite unfitted for any career except art, and so I cut Latin, Algebra, high mathematics and substituted dramatics instead.

I took him frequently to Paris Picture Galleries, dress shows, etc., to give an insight into all sides of art.

We traveled a great deal to all parts of the world and, while in different countries, I let Peter play with any children he met on the beaches, always provided they had clean noses and no spots. His tutor or governess was completely disgusted at this order! Peter never had any of the usual children's ailments due, I believe, to a great extent his cleanliness. He was made to gargle twice daily, also after coming out of the swimming pool or sea. His hands were washed in a disinfectant before each meal. A hot bath— no shower— morning and evening— and his hair washed three times weekly. He had no inoculation— except the 91st Psalm!— he was vaccinated at three-days-old— a terrific arm resulting.

When we went to Majorca, we leased a royal estate complete with furnishings and servants. We also had Peter's tutor, my maid and the General's manservant. Such a lovely place; the General always loved it there.

One evening, as we dressed and went out to dinner, Peter bowed low to a lady who was sitting at the next table. He greeted her with "How do you do?" So charmed with his gentlemanly behavior, she invited him to her table after we had finished eating. Later, when he rejoined the General and me, he excitedly told how she was on the Titanic when it sank.

"Oh, pshaw," said I, but the General expressed plausibility.

As time went on, we grew to enjoy the lady's company and conversation immensely. It seems that she was American-born of the Virginia family of Russells— Edith was her first name, and was traveling from Southampton to New York when she rode the famous Titanic.

Once when we were staying in Cuba's largest hotel, I put Peter in the hotel's pool since he was an excellent swimmer. I always wear a black bathing dress; it looked so good next to my white skin. Anyway, he came to me— I was reading in the garden— for seventy-five cents charged for his swimming. In a moment, he returned because he was charged each time he got out.

Cuba is the biggest gyp of all. I bought a large quantity of my favorite perfume, Mary Guest, because of the low price and no duty. On return sail, I asked if Peter and the General liked my perfume. They couldn't smell it— it was plain liquid!

I remember an incident once in Port Said which is quite a lovely place. Nevertheless, there is part of the port which is inhabited by homosexuals. People like us would recognize them as such in only a moment. Anyway, there was an acquaintance of mine who was searching for the harbor master for business matters. Well, it seemed the harbor master lived in this particular district. My acquaintance, while searching, became lost and finally told a man on the street, "I've got to find somebody!"

The man jumped at the statement and quickly asked, "Sure, do you want him tall or short, blond or dark, or just what?"

Oh no," my friend said. "I want the harbor master."

"The harbor master!" the man exclaimed, thinking what appeal could that burly old man have for my friend. Then he added slyly, "It may be difficult, but I think it can be arranged."

Once, when we were bored with the Bahamas, we decided to go to Australia. We— the General, Peter and I— were accompanied by my French maid, Peter's tutor and the General's manservant. I was trying to be economical, as the cost of the trip was quite expensive. Peter could go at half-fare and still have a stateroom if only he would eat with the children instead of eating with us at the captain's table. So this was agreed.

On this first evening of the voyage, Peter put on his suit tailored by the King's tailor and silk stockings up to his knees— he was six at the time. He turned around three times for my examination and then departed for the children's dining room.

In only a matter of moments, he returned asking if he might use the telephone. I consented, but I asked about his abrupt return from dinner. He was going to call for room service since he refused to eat with the children. He explained that the poorly-dressed kids sat around an unattended table where they were to serve themselves from bowls. Two boys each stuffed their mouths with minced chicken and mashed potatoes and slowly let it ooze out on their plate. Tiring of this, they staged a contest of who could spit milk out the greatest distance. At this, Peter had returned to our stateroom and exclaimed, "I'd rather not eat than have dinner with these little barbarians." So we made the proper adjustment with the captain as to the fare and Peter ate with us at the captain's table. The captain was both annoyed and amazed at Peter's proper manners.

His artistic sense often overcame his sense of right and wrong. For instance, he climbed up the mast of a visiting Man-of-War on one hot day in Cannes. While a voluble and perspiring Marie, the cook— it being the tutor's day off— captain and crew shouted at him in various languages from the deck below, he refused to descend though the departure bell for visitors had rung. On being questioned afterward, his excuse was "the lights on the water were so beautiful." That and other things decided me to give "Master Peter" a good talking to. I did so, and our conversation ended on this note: "Yes, Mum, I know— I'm honestly terribly sorry! I guess I was 'off the straight and narrow path' for a bit, but it was fun to stretch my legs!"

When Peter was quite young, he brought a friend home to dinner. The General and I were quite pleased at his new friend. When later I asked about the lad, Peter said. "Oh, that silly shit!" I quickly spoke to him without raising an eyebrow. I told him not to use the word in the company of women, but that it was quite all right in a group of men.

When Peter was still young, he would slip around to the ashtrays and smoke the leftover "stubs" of cigarettes. The servants told me of his little habit. So I bought some special cigarettes and decided to use my own special brand of psychology. I called Peter in and told him that I did not want him smoking our guests' cigarettes stubs, warning him of mouth sores and cancer. "Now, if you must smoke, don't smoke ladies cigarettes; smoke a man's cigarette." I then offered him a Semolia— a strong asthmatic cigarette. After a puff or two, he said he much preferred the ladies' brand. However, he would do without rather than smoke the *man's* cigarette.

I used the same technique to break Peter of drinking. When he was only seven-years-old, Peter had a bad habit of drinking the remains of our guests' drinks after a party. I was aware of his habit; in fact, I watched him down more than a quart of drink "residue" after one party. I waited for him to get tipsy or something. He must have an iron digestive tract! It didn't faze him. Finally, the servants came to me, saying, "Master Peter is becoming an alcoholic."

At the next large cocktail— oh, about ninety— party the General and I gave, I instructed the servants to put emetic tablets in some of the drink remainders. Of course, Peter drank the drink leftovers. A little later, I heard him going "Hhhrump— hhhrrrump." Such terrible heaving!

Peter was born with the curse of hay fever and every summer, the flowers in our house or apartment were taboo. Sometimes he got so ill we had to send him to the seaside for the month of August. During such a bout, I was at a party in Paris and ran into a friend who said, "Why so depressed?" I explained that Peter was so ill with hay fever that he was in Cannes. She said, "I suppose you've tried everything?"

I said, "Yes," so her reply was, "Why not give God a chance?" and gave me a card to a Christian Science practitioner in London.

On our return, I sent Peter to her, explaining that we were *not* Christian Scientists but Church of England. After about six visits to that practitioner, Peter returned one day carrying a huge bunch of pinks. I gasped, "No sleep for anyone tonight— only sneeze, sneeze, sneeze."

"Oh no," said Peter. "We've trodden on the devil and no more hay fever." He proceeded to say the Scientific Statement of Being, his face buried in the flowers. Never since that day has he been troubled with hay fever.

After that, he became an usher in the Christian Science Church, but he later returned to his original religion in which he was baptized.

Of course he was baptized in the Church of England, but he had governesses and tutors who were of all nationalities— a German Jewess, a Spanish atheist, an Italian Roman Catholic. I made them explain their faiths to Peter and personally told him about Buddhism and various Indian sects. He attended services in churches, cathedrals, synagogues and for some time was usher in a Christian Science Sunday School, as I said.

So at seven-years-old, he got the idea that the true religion— as he explained it— "was like a wheel, with all the spokes running into the hub which is God and all the spokes— the various religions— have different names."

His religious convictions often landed him in trouble and on board ship he refused to play with the little girl because she was dressed in denim slacks.

"She's an abomination unto the Lord!" said Peter. "It says so plainly in the twenty-second chapter of Deuteronomy." Needless to say the rather young mother thought him crazy, but I did not insist.

Yes, I learned a lot of my religion from Peter— tolerance, kindness and the ability to see the other fellow's point of view. After all, it's not astonishing, for in the Guide Book of Life, it says, "A little child shall lead them."

I was born a member of the Church of England and I shall die a member of the Church of England! Up until a few years ago, I continued to attend St. Alban's Episcopal Church; I always sat in the third pew on the left side. However, I quit attending because one Sunday a mother inappropriately dressed with two young— about five and seven years old— children and including a baby in a plastic tray sat next to me. During the entire service, the children ran rampant, stumbling all over me, dropping prayer books, and they ran up the aisle during the Lord's Prayer, speaking and calling to each other. All the time the mother was itchy-gitchy-goo with the baby in the plastic tray. I could barely hear the service. At the end of the service, I went up for communion; the woman sat the baby in the plastic dish beside me. It smelled to high heavens; you know babies run at both ends!

Since the father had often been a guest in our home and he had officiated at the General's funeral, I decided to freely discuss the matter with him. The Bishop— he always sponged it up at our cocktail parties. Once the maid said the Bishop had drunk nine cocktails and wanted more. I said to tell the bartender (we got him from Romanoff's), "No more for the Bishop!" Anyway, totally unsympathetic to my idea of having no children allowed to the services, he brushed me off with the Scripture: Suffer little children come unto me.

A sort of depression hit us and the General said we had lost our wealth. From then on we had to economize. At that time, we had three large homes in different parts of England. We were to keep only the one house in London; we were to dismiss all servants— even my French maid and the General's manservant. Knowing it might be my last time, I asked the General's permission to go to Paris for my fittings of some already-bought clothes— Dior and Mainbacher. Peter was to go with me and his tutor— oh, dear, we also had to discharge the tutor who was a charming young Oxford student. Anyway, he could go on this trip.

Once in Paris, I told the young tutor to go on about his sightseeing and having fun— I enjoyed being kind and understanding to our help— while I would watch after Peter myself. Peter was about nine-years-old then and he was downstairs at our hotel playing with some German children. Suddenly there was a terrific crash and the tinkling of broken glass; I rushed to find Peter next to a broken French door with his right arm covered with blood. The arm had been slit almost the full length of the arm— from shoulder to wrist. That evening, the French doctor told me that he felt it best to remove the arm at the shoulder socket. Oh, my goodness, Peter would never be able to shoot, ride, *anything*. The doctor told me that we must talk to Peter gently and make him understand that gangrene was probably setting in and the operation should be early the next morning. The mere mention of the idea set Peter in a rage.

"You are not taking my arm off; you are not even touching my arm. I am religious; I believe in God and God will not let such a thing happen to me. If Faith can move mountains, then keeping my arm is a small thing in comparison. So you, *monsieur le docteur,* can go jump in the lake and drown yourself!" Peter exclaimed. That was that.

Peter could not be moved from the hotel and we had two full-time nurses; one who was French and one was English— American really. Peter's English was not so good at that time. I called the General to tell him of the situation. He had been offered two new regiments and was preparing to take leadership. I told him the specialist had advised that we take Peter to Florida or California as soon as he could be moved because those climates were best for what he had. The General agreed to resign his commission and help with Peter, since I, too, must go to America since we could no longer afford a nurse.

While Peter was still recovering, I told him that he had been invited to join the Queen's Guard, a great honor, but now what could he do? Naturally he was rejected by all armies which was a cause of sadness to all three of us. He is very proud of his long connection with the army, on my side since 1100, and the fact that he had ancestors on both sides in the famous battle of Waterloo.

Peter's face brightened and he said, "I'm not sorry this happened; in fact, I'm glad it happened. I never wanted to be a soldier; I think it's wrong to fight and kill people."

This, in particular, displeased the General who had planned for Peter a military career. Well, the arm accident ended all of that.

Peter continued, "I want to be an actor and now I can be." You cannot imagine how the General felt when Peter told him of his idea for the future.

"An actor— my son a common jester with a cap and bells, dancing and prancing around in front of people!"

After Peter's arm was smashed and slashed by the window, his plans to go into the Queen's Royal Guard was dashed. This gave fuel to his wish to become an actor. The General's sister, Lady Evanston, who later became the Honorable Mrs. Lubbock, threw her hands up in disgust. "My nephew a jester with a silly cap and prancing around! I want no part of him," she continued. By her marriage, she had inherited untold millions that her husband, king of the stock exchange, had amassed. Previously, she had planned to give all to Peter, making him perhaps one of the wealthiest— if not *the* wealthiest— lad in all England. This is what Peter gave up to become an actor.

It was on the ship Bremen that the General, Peter and I came to America. Earlier, on this ship, Peter conquered some of his bashfulness. Although Peter was only seven or eight years of age, he was a lovely dancer. After tiring of dancing with him, I asked to remain seated. Peter said, "Mother, who can I dance with?"

I said, "Why don't you ask the Queen of Spain?"

He was a bit standoffish at asking the royal co-passenger; then he went to her and bowed lowly and asked, "Would Her Majesty bain to dance with me?"

Amused and charmed by such a young gentleman's request, she gladly consented.

Now that we were living in Palm Beach, Peter announced once again that he wanted to become an actor. Always before, we sort of humored him. Even at four, he would ask if he could invite an audience to see him after dinner. So I'd have the butler, the General's manservant, my French maid and the kitchen help join the General and me to form his audience. Then he would dance and sing and act. I shall not forget the song he composed and sang:

> *There was a little boy*
> *who was born to fight war*
> *but he wanted to become*
> *an actor because he*
> *he didn't believe in wars.*

This, in particular, displeased the General, who had planned for Peter a military career. Well, the arm accident ended all of that. Of course, I sympathized with Peter's ambitions because I always wanted to be an actress. But, remember, my father had said, "There's not a lady in the theatre. Go immediately to your room and read about Jezebel in the Bible!"

One time when the General and I were returning to our place in Palm Beach, Florida, we were just past the narrow bridge coming from the line of hotels in Miami Beach. As we stopped at a traffic light, the General commented on the young girl on the bicycle standing next to us who was giving him the eye. Just a moment or two later, the bicycle wavered a bit and the girl leaped into the air. She fell to the ground; her books remained strapped to the bicycle's front fender. The service station attendants rushed to her rescue and I carefully pulled our Cadillac over to the curb nearby. The girl showed no marks of injury, but she claimed that our automobile had hit her.

The next day, her parents called, announcing that they were suing the General and me. "Preposterous!" the General exclaimed, since we had not touched the girl— so he went to the head of the Miami Police. The police said the service station attendant testified against us and that we should pay the out-of-court sum. The General pulled a big "string" or two; an investigation followed and revealed that the whole thing was a racket which had been going on for several years.

America is such a beautiful place. The climate is marvelous and the buildings are the nicest in the world. But the only thing wrong is the American people. It seems that they don't know anything and they won't ask.

What was that short blonde actor's name? I used to call him "Stick
'Em Up"— oh, yes, Alan Ladd. His wife was an agent by the name of
Sue Carol— whoever Sue Carol is supposed to be. Anyway, she called
me about having Peter work in a film. You Americans have some law
about a parent or guardian signing contracts for an actor who is a
minor. So she wanted to purchase his acting services from MGM.
Later she called back saying that they would lose money on Peter—
that sixty thousand dollars was too much to spend on him. I agreed
with her and said, "By all means, don't lose money on him."

She said, "Well, you know that actors with English accents are a
dime a dozen!"

That's— "actors with English accents are a dime a dozen"— not
what Arthur J. Rank told Peter. He said, "Why go to America? You
can write your own ticket here in England!"

Louis B. Mayer felt the same way. He gave Peter a double contract
because, even as a newcomer, he recognized Peter as having "class."

I had never heard the word used that way before. L. B. said he
wished that he himself could have Peter's "meticulous dress and
impeccable manners." It was no wonder that he said "he has class"
when he was comparing Peter to red-soxed Van Johnson and gum-
chewing Mickey Rooney!

After all, Peter was not a rank amateur. Back when Peter was only
seven-years-old, he made his debut in an English film called "Old
Bill." Look at this cute picture of him beside that locomotive. He
quickly became sort of a British Jackie Coogan. Little wonder old
Mayer grabbed Peter up now for the very English "Lord Jeff."

That Louis B. Mayer! He was such a nice man. Did you know that
he used to be a garbage collector in Halifax? He told me all about his
life— like how he was educated in night school. He was always asking
me questions— somewhat like picking my brain. He would allow me
to slap him around and say what I thought.

One particular time, I remember when he had ridden a horse and
fallen. He had a bad leg injury. Nevertheless, one day when Peter and
I entered his office with some other people, he just spoke to us
without standing up. Very quickly I snorted, "We all know that you
have a leg injury, but at least you may acknowledge my presence by a
slight tilting of your body!"

Once Mrs. Temple invited Peter and me to a party for Shirley. Shirley, with over-long curls and a pretty party smock, was a terribly arrogant and haughty child.

"This party is just for you, Peter," she said. She explained this remark later when they posed for photographs together: "My other friends, who might have come, feel that you are beneath them. However, even though you aren't a star, I don't mind posing with you."

Later, when Peter's English and French popularity became known in America, several major motion picture companies bid huge amounts for Peter. Shirley Temple, who all associates agreed needed her bottom spanked, said, "Oh, they— the movie companies— are just doing it because of my influence."

At that tender age, she was already fading.

That Elizabeth Taylor! Such a lovely girl. English, you know. Always she has such nice elocution and diction. After all, she was reared somewhat like Peter. I remember when she and her parents arrived on the Queen Mary not long before Elizabeth made "Lassie Come Home" with Peter and "National Velvet."

When Liz and Peter played together in "Little Women," Mrs. Taylor would say, "Look at them; they are both such pretty children."

Once when Peter was over at Metro-Goldwyn-Mayer to sign a contract with Louis B. Mayer, when I served as his advisor, Elizabeth was there. She was such a pretty child. Anyway, Peter went to his dressing room and there she sat in the corner of it. He refused to sign the contract until "that brat" was removed from his dressing room. He said later she was a lot of bull.

Peter chose to ignore Elizabeth's party invitations. He once called Lana Turner "an easy girl to forget." Maybe he found Liz the same at that time.

That Van Johnson— I know about him! Anyway, every Sunday, the General and I, with Peter, would attend St. Alban's Episcopal church in Westwood. Oh, it's the Church of England on UCLA campus. One day Peter was telling Van that he had to miss some occasion because he attended church. Van said, "To go to church is sissy, but to go to church with your parents is doubly sissy!" Then Peter quit going; I kept on going.

Homosexual Peter tried hard to be thought one— by being persistently with Van Johnson— even after he met trouble and was bailed out. Louis B. Mayer sent for me and asked if Peter was one. I mentioned their friendship (?). Instead of giving him the standard treatment of hysterics, I said, "You spent thousands on Judy Garland to find out if she is a dope addict! Send Peter to Menninger's and in one day they'll test his glands and you've got 'yes' or 'no'— a medical fact." I never said he was one, nor do I think so.

Shortly— oh, maybe three or four years after we brought Peter to California, I became subject to a terrible condition. Every time someone said something nice to me, I would go to my room and cry. Then, if I dropped a cup, I would just go all to pieces. I was blue and depressed; sometimes I was crabby and very irritable. Something just had to be done.

Finally, I went to the French doctor named Bethea. He examined me and said that I was fine down there. "Why," he said, "you're like an eighteen-year-old girl there. You can have at least ten more children!"

"No thanks," I told him. "I've got one brat and I don't want another. I hate babies; they run and smell at both ends."

Anyway, he finally offered me the hysterectomy for fifteen hundred dollars. Since the British doctors seem to give so much more care to their patients, the General and I flew to England. The doctors there did not wish to operate, but they at least agreed to for two thousand dollars. That's a hell of a lot to get rid of a human baby-box!

Back to California we jetted. I called a surgeon at St. John's in Santa Monica. "What are you doing Thursday morning? Well, then, I'll be over about six o'clock and we'll yank that thing out and throw it in the garbage."

I was in the expensive Louis B. Mayer suite. With my baby-box in the garbage, I was ready to go home, but the doctor said I must wait fifteen days. So up out of bed I got and climbed out the window and drove home. Why do women need those things? I've felt wonderful ever since!

Peter learned to drive a car in Ceylon and shoot with a rifle at the age of ten. At eleven he was inclined to be aggressive— he blacked the eyes and badly lamed a sixteen-year-old bellhop in a London hotel for some fancied insult. I pointed out to him that only people of low education and a still lower background and conception of life lose control of their emotions and descend to brute force, and that "gentleness was the sign of a gentleman." He saw it after a bit, apologized to the boy and gave him six of his best records. After that, he had boxing lessons which took some of the steam out of him.

Peter adores animals— but likes a kennel man to look after them. He is the soul of kindness, but if you are ill, don't expect any "sitting-by-your-bed" business. He'll say how sorry he is with books and flowers.

He is the most *undomesticated* person on earth! He likes to keep his thumb on a bell— how the maids complained of this! He loves a well-run house, but how it gets like that is a complete mystery to him. Gardening, bedmaking, washing up all just happen and, being ultra-British, that's the maid's job.

On Sunday morning, February 15, 1953, the General awoke very early complaining of pains in the lower abdomen. I got up and got him aspirin and a cup of hot tea; I then called his doctor— a Frenchman by the name of Dr. (hic) Bouchet. He asked what I had done for the General and then sarcastically asked why I had called for him. "Do I have to teach you *everything* about your profession?" I retorted.

Later, he came over and, after fixing himself a drink, proceeded to examine the ailing General. Upon lowering the covers, we found the General had a double hernia which, because of its protruding, looked the size of a fist. Once outside, the doctor said, "We must take (hic) him to the hospital immediately and (hic) prepare him for surgery."

"Absolutely not," I said. "Do you want him to die? If he must, he will die in peace."

I then said that since the General was already past ninety years old, he probably wouldn't even survive the anesthesia. The doctor left in a huff, but not before fixing himself a quick one for the road.

The General got up and prepared for a car ride— at that time we had three Cadillacs; one for each one of us. However, he didn't quite feel up to it. So I said, "Let's just sit here in the garden and talk, if you like— or would you rather go to bed?" I never let him feel like a helpless invalid. So we sat in the garden and talked.

I especially remember one statement that he made during that last conversation. "Peter is bound to marry beneath him." (And sure enough, it happened!) He asked me who had been chosen the chairman of the United Empire Party. He said he regretted his causing me to leave this position and that he was very proud of me. He further said, "a good wife you have been, but you've been so much more. You've always gone beyond the call of duty." With that comment, he fell asleep— the deep sleep of death.

It was about noon-day and I immediately called that drinking French doctor and he begrudgingly came. After a drink, he declared the General dead. "You think I need you to tell me that! I've seen hundreds of dead people during the plague of India. What I want is the name of a good beauty parlor for the General," I said.

Peter had been told by the doctor that the General might die at any time and not to be too far away. However, Peter wanted to go to Hawaii and he went. Now began my struggle to notify Peter of his father's death. Many anxious hours and fourteen long distance phone calls later, I finally got through to him. He simply said, "Keep him on ice until Saturday."

I said that the mortuary wouldn't keep the body past Saturday— there was some kind of law. So Peter came in on Friday night. We went down and selected the casket. That shyster undertaker tried to sell me an expensive bronze casket. How foolish! It wasn't necessary that the famous general be buried in the most expensive casket. Besides, the Union Jack would cover most of it.

Of course, the *Times* of London, *Daily Mirror* and others called me for an account of the General's death. I said, "He died quietly and peacefully." That was all. It was a military funeral conducted with only a graveside service in Inglewood. After the service, I saluted the coffin— the proper protocol for the wife of a general; Peter did not. I did not shed a tear. That evening Peter was going out. He asked me what I would do for dinner. Then he took me to a small place on Sepulveda Boulevard and buried his face in a newspaper while I ate. He then went out on the town.

I still remember as we drove to the mortuary to select a casket, he turned the radio to some loud, jivey music. When I commented on it, Peter said, "Yes, the music is quite fitting for the General— it's 'Adios'." So I was alone in the house on Sunset Boulevard the night of   the funeral. The next day Peter flew to New York.

Peter has such a snobbish air when it comes to giving autographs to fans. At one time, there were thousands of requests a week for auto-graphed pictures. Now there are still some. Bonnie Williams, down at the Chrislaw Productions office uses a rubber stamp on the pictures.

Once, at a premiere, I saw Peter snub his fans' requests for auto-graphs. I took him aside and reminded him that he had come down in the world. "Peter, you're no longer a candidate for the Queen's Royal Guard; these people don't know you as the son of a general and grandson of a general. You are now a working man that these people pay an admission to see in a movie. You owe it to them to grant them autographs."

However, he never enjoyed the custom and only did so according to his moods. It is said that he now pays six hundred dollars a month to keep his name and pictures out of newspapers and magazines.

My son Peter is a very complex character. He had a horror of being thought young. An idea that he might need advice was anathema to him. Even after he grew up, I saw traces of adolescence in him. For instance, he never sits, he sprawls; he never likes to say where he is going. During his early years and even later years, he was and still is influenced to a certain extent, by the last person he is with. Mickey Rooney and Frank Sinatra are examples of his influenced behavior. God, the nights I had to call Mickey's mother to ask if he were staying overnight with Mickey. Mickey was a darling "Puck," but not my choice of a companion for Peter. All were signs of "See, I've grown up and off the chain." The British have a lovely custom of giving a gold house key to represent the change from boyhood to manhood.

If it is someone he likes, Peter is all smiles and it delights my heart; but if he has been in the society of some "pseudo" sophisticate who regards parents as God's method for entering the world to be quickly forgotten, he is moody and distraught. Unlike most of the movie stars, Peter had led a life more luxurious than that he has today so that there should be no danger of his "money"— oh, what a vulgar term!—or possessions going to his head.

Many years ago, Peter was so loyal and reliable. When the General and I found it difficult to rent a house, Peter decided to buy a cottage at 11571 Sunset Boulevard. It was too small for us— but, oh, how we enjoyed the lovely garden. Every friend that Peter had, particularly most married women, said, "Don't do it." "A millstone around your neck." "The up-keep is terrific," and so on and so forth. He disregarded them and we— the General and I— were for many years "welcome guests" with an only child whose welfare and success was a never-ending source of interest and pleasure. The General adored Peter and enjoyed some happiness in those years. Thank God the General did not live longer however!

Chapter Four
Patricia Kennedy— The Bride, The Bitch

Patricia Lawford is a bitch. She really is such a bitch. Look how she trapped Peter. After all, Peter was used to women throwing themselves at him; sex on a silver platter. I often found male contraceptives in his bedroom among his things. I never said anything; then they would disappear. He probably flushed them down the toilet in some girl's apartment. But not Pat Kennedy's!

Jack Kennedy introduced Patricia to Peter in Palm Beach. Peter would bump into her all over the world. He met her in Chicago when he was supporting Eisenhower— did you know that Eisenhower was a Mid-West farmboy? Is it true that money bought him into West Point? When Patricia Kennedy came to visit, she took a suite at the Bel-Air Hotel and had Cardinal McIntyre as her chaperone. When Peter and she said good night, it was in the lobby and done with a hand shake: "Good night, Mr. Lawford."

Even Cardinal McIntyre chaperoned Patricia and Peter on the jet when she went to Hong Kong. Have you ever heard of such? I asked her, "Do you think Peter will rape you on the plane?" One thing I'm sure of— she was a virgin. I always told Peter that the girl he should marry should be a piece of white paper on which he should be the first mark. That Sharman Douglas always threw herself at him as did Princess Ira von Furstenburg. I never cared for either one.

When I gave an engagement party for my friends in honor of Patricia and Peter, I shall not forget what a bitch she was. I suppose there were seventy-five guests all asking where the prospective bride was. When she did show up, nearly two hours later, she was in sports attire. She insisted that Peter go out with her somewhere that very moment. When I asked if she did not wish to meet Peter's friends, she said, "No, not now. Tell them that I'm not feeling well."

They then went out to dinner. That bitch! But, oh, what a pretty girl.

Before Peter's wedding, I was invited to lunch *alone* with Mr. Kennedy at the Plaza in New York. When I met old Joe Kennedy previous to Peter's marriage to Patricia Kennedy, he exclaimed, "My beautiful daughter wants to marry a non-Catholic, a Britisher, and an actor— oh no!" I didn't like old Kennedy's appearance, his background, his manners or his speech. Old Joe repeated a former statement: "If there's anything I think I'd hate as a son-in-law, it's an actor; and if there's anything I think I'd hate worse than an actor as a son-in-law, it's an English actor."

I wish you could have seen his mouth fall when I said, "We've got lots of old fuddy-duddies in England, I'm sorry to say, but none like you! You're an old fuddy-duddy, an old fogey and I want nothing more to do with you." I immediately arose to leave without even eating lunch. That was that. What else was I to say after he insulted my English-born son? Why that barefoot Irish peasant!

Later I was invited to a dinner *alone* with Mrs. Joseph Kennedy. This etiquette is quite incorrect.

At the pre-wedding dinner the night before the wedding, I was not allowed my correct place as the mother of the groom. I was not seated at either the long table or next to Mr. Joe Kennedy, nor was I seated at the side of the eldest son (then Senator John Kennedy). Instead, I was seated in a corner at a table for two with the officiating priest— I am *not* a Roman Catholic. When dinner was over, none of the family noticed me enough to say goodbye; so I left for my hotel alone while they all went to a night club.

I met one sister— Eunice Shriver— when she invited me to a pre-wedding dinner party. There Senator Kennedy introduced himself; otherwise, I met none of them. The whole attitude was to treat me as a "poor relation," to be tolerated while the wedding was proceeding and then forgotten. No one made an effort to talk to me or even make me feel at home or welcome. If it had not been for my friends, Prince Franzi and Princess Stephanie Hohenlohe, I would have been isolated there in New York.

And if it had not been for my good friends, Prince and Princess Hohenhole and others, I should have had a miserable time at Peter and Patricia Lawford's wedding. I felt like a cook who was permitted to see the "wedding of the young master."

I did not walk out as I was advised by the Hohenholes, as I did not want any fuss at the wedding of my only child who is very dear to me. Many advised me to walk out, but imagine the headlines in the London papers. I just would not— I couldn't do it for the publicity for Peter. A peasant I am not!

No, Peter never became a Catholic to marry Patricia Kennedy. However, they did request that he become an American citizen. I have many wonderful American friends; I love the climate here. But I am a British subject. My home address is London, England. I do not reside in Beverly Hills. Don't speak to me of Blue Book society registers. No, no, no! I've told you I do not want to be in the Beverly Hills Blue Book. I'm in Debrett's of England. And Debrett's Peerage is over a hundred and fifty years old. Ah, here it is:

Lawford, Lady— *May Sommerville, da. of Col. F.W. Bunny, late Roy Berks. Regt.: m. 1924, as his second wife, Lieut. -Gen. Sir Sidney Turing Barlow Lawford, K.C.B. who d. 1953. 1350, Midvale Av. W. Los Angeles, California USA 90024*

The wedding itself was held April 24, 1954, at the Roman Catholic Church of St. Thomas More in New York, as you can see by this invitation. There must have been about two hundred and fifty people there— mostly the Kennedy's social friends and Peter's movie friends. The people I brought to the wedding— Prince Alexander of Greece, Prince and Princess Hohenhole, etc., etc.— were the only titled people there. One funny thing— about thirty or forty housewives slipped in early and saw the entire ceremony— it only lasted a few minutes and was performed by a Notre Dame president named Cavanaugh. He was the same bore that I had sat with the night before at the pre-wedding dinner.

Patricia, who was given in marriage by Old Joe, was a beautiful bride. Her gown was lovely and she smiled radiantly. She was the prettiest of the Kennedy girls. I think her sister Jean attended— didn't she marry a chap named Smith? Patricia's brothers, Jack, Bobby and Teddy, served as ushers. The press said that Peter forgot to kiss Patricia at the end of the marriage ceremony, but Peter did not kiss her because he knew it would be in poor taste.

Oh, what a crush outside of the church. At least twenty policemen— one here and one here and one here— held back a crowd of three thousand. They had been forced to block off the street between Park Avenue and what was that other street? Madison?

Anyway. We finally managed to get to the reception at the Plaza. It was in the Terrace Room and the whole of the room was beautifully decorated. Red roses here and there and everywhere— banks of them. And, of course, there again was the long family table where I should have been seated— the Kennedys are not too hot on protocol!

The Kennedy women had on big picture hats— lovely, but not suitable for the occasion. Jean Kennedy wore a pink and blue print taffeta gown with a large blue picture hat. Quite incorrect. I wore a small off-the-face chapeau just like the Queen wears. On public occasions, a true lady never covers her face from cameras or from people who wish to see her face.

Look at Rose Kennedy's dress in this picture! It looks as if she bought it right off the peg. I'm sure that she got it off the rack at Bloomingdale's. You would think that she would select more carefully for her daughter's wedding. But look at my dress— oh, I wish the pictures in this album were in color! My dress was the most beautiful shade of blue— kind of a Dior blue. Waldo, who did some designing for MGM, was a dear friend of mine and he designed the dress for me. I wonder where Waldo is now?

I've called Rose Kennedy "Me Too" since the wedding reception. The newspaper photographer kept wanting to get a photograph of me wearing my lovely dress. Every time they would get me aside to pose, Rose would come barging in screeching in a high-pitched voice, "Me too— Me too!" There was no way that the photographer could photograph me without "Me Too."

There's Greer Garson— she was so good in "Mrs. Miniver" — and she was a friend of Peter's. I didn't care much for her, but I adored her husband, Buddy— Buddy Fogelson, who has all that oil down in Texas or somewhere.

And that's Nina Anderton in that reception picture. She called me up and said, "Oh, May, can't you get me an invitation to Peter's wedding? I'd be so grateful."

You know, she does a lot of nice work for the City of Hope— she gives them thousands and thousands of dollars. Nina has the loveliest collection of diamonds— I've always admired them, but she wears them in poor taste. Why, once, at a luncheon, she had big diamonds at her ears, at her neck, on her arms, everywhere diamonds! Absolutely vulgar! Her house in Bel-air has been robbed several times, but she doesn't seem to mind. Oh, but what was I saying: Nina Anderton was begging me for an invitation to Peter's wedding— where is she now?

No, I never see her anymore except her picture on the society page of the newspapers— when the big cocktail parties with the magnums of champagne stop, they all disappear.

Marion Davies was at the wedding and the reception. Such a sweet dear— I really liked her— so kind and generous. Did you ever hear the story of her bringing almost the entire congregation from church home with her for luncheon? Well, the cook, who had prepared the table for six people, took off her apron and said, "Miss Marion, I quit!"

So many people whisper that Marion and that newspaperman Hearst were the real mother and father to Patricia Van Cleve,

Dagwood's wife— no, I mean, Mrs. Arthur Lake. I must ask Patrick Mahony— he would know the truth.

I think that it was Patrick who helped Marion— she was *so* drunk— to her chauffeured limousine at the reception. Poor Marion, I always felt sorry for her— what an awful way to die. I heard that she had throat cancer and that they were treating her with cobalt. One day a young doctor— not her regular one— gave her too much cobalt and she died of a charred and blackened throat. Poor Marion.

You remember I told you a little about dancing with Jack Kennedy. I had met him before at his sister's house before the wedding day. Anyway, during the wedding reception, he watched all the dancers. There were eight hundred people there at the Plaza. I was dancing with somebody else 'round the room. He came over on crutches and tapped the person's shoulder and then asked them to relinquish me. You see, that's the way it 'tis.

"Well," I said, "Am I supposed to dance with you?"

"Yes."

"On the end of these sticks?"

"I'm getting rid of them. I hear you're the best *danzer* in the room."

"Never believe everything you hear, Sonny." And with that, I grabbed the crutches. I can be damned patronizing if I like. You know what I mean?

"Here," I said, and I handed him the sticks.

"Throw them down," he responded, "we don't need them." Then he stood up like that— sort of swaying on his feet and then he grabbed hold of my...

"Listen, Sonny," I said, "this is a wedding; you're going to turn in into your funeral. Your face looks like unbaked bread. Go into the buffet and ask them to give you a jigger of brandy and put a jigger of champagne on top of it— a Sir Roger's Pag. Drink it down and you'll be all right."

"A Roger's Plague?"

"Roger's Pag, P-A-G."

"Where did you learn that?"

"India."

"You don't want to dance anymore?"

"You call it dancing; I call it gymnastics. Goodbye."
I never saw him again.

Immediately after Peter's wedding, I went to visit Princess Stephanie Hohenhole and her darling son, Franzi, in Philadelphia. They were quite uppity-up in Philadelphia society and they loved it there. Such a dinner party that Franzi gave for me with thirty-five members of the town's top society attending. The newspapers lauded the affair in glowing terms.

Later, Stephanie went to Washington to live. She was so miserable, lonely and unhappy. A letter from Franzi came the same day that one arrived from his mother, telling how she needed an escort for parties and a dance partner.

Did I know someone? Well, at the moment I was seeing David Reed, who had some governmental position in Washington, but often was in Los Angeles. Always he saw me when he was here and every week there were letters from him when he was away. So I said that he was rich, well bred, a good dancer and single. So very soon, David became Steph's escort. He stopped visiting me and also calling or writing. The next thing I knew, I had a letter from the two of them from their place in London. This time they wanted a letter of introduction into London society circles. I gave them a letter to this son of an important general— Morgan was the name— and I suppose they went on from there. Later I got a postcard with a cat on the front. "This made me think of you. David," was the entire message.

Patricia Lawford has millions— Old Joe is supposed to have given each of his children ten million dollars when they reached twenty-one years of age— so I think Patricia has ten million of her own. But still Peter pays all the bills. Mrs. Lawford keeps her money put away, and lets him spend his. Now what do you think of that?

My son and daughter-in-law live in a very nice house once owned by Louis B. Mayer. It's a million-dollar beach house at 625 Ocean Ave. in Santa Monica. The house has many rooms— I especially like the room with the red leather walls and a movie screen that appeared out of nowhere. There is a marble swimming pool and a lovely rose garden adjoining.

At the christening of my first grandchild— Christopher Kennedy Lawford, after whom Peter named Chrislaw Productions— I was invited to the church, but was completely omitted from the after-church reception. The second christening— my granddaughter Sydney, so named for the General— I accidentally happened to hear about by sitting next to Jimmy Durante at a dinner party, who said he was godfather! He asked me, "Why were you not there?" At the third christening— Victoria Francis— "Victoria" because her Uncle Jack that same day won re-election as a Senator, and "Francis" for Peter's close friend Frank Sinatra— I was invited to both church and reception because the gossip was so intense about the previous one.

Mrs. Lawford and the children never have been in my house, although I frequently invite them. I invited the children to a small party at my house. Mrs. Lawford said, "Much too far away"— it was eight minutes from their door to my door— regardless of the fact that they are often flown to Florida, Lake Tahoe and Boston.

Once, while Patricia and Peter were away, I thought I'd go and see the children. The butler reluctantly let me in. Just then the French governess, who recognized me and seemed pleased to see me, brought them in to see me. They were most attractive children to look at and were well mannered— Pat Lawford should be complimented for this.

But they were a bit timid; they looked at me as if I was very funny. The butler said, "Say how do you do, Lady Lawford."

The little boy said, "How do you do, Lady Lawford."

Then the little girl curtsied and said, "How do you do, Lady Lawford."

Then the little one— about two or three years old, tried to curtsey and fell right on her bottom.

I said, "Come up on my lap and give me a big fat kiss. I'm your grandmother."

The small boy said, "We know your name is May because when they talk about you, they call you May."

"But you can call me grandmother," I said to them.

"No thank you," they said. "We already have one grandmother. She's very beautiful and very rich and has five houses."

I said, "I am your grandmother, too."

The children said, "Thank you so much, but we already have one. We don't want another grandmother."

I have not bothered them since.

I wonder why Patricia Lawford dines alone now at the Colony? Has she no friends or acquaintances to dine with? Did you see where she was refused entrance to the Oak Room of the Savoy? I think it was because she had on such short shorts. Can you imagine her going to dinner in such attire? Why does she do it? Is it her way of getting attention? She certainly can't desire such tasteless publicity. I often wondered if she married Peter to get her name in the papers all the time. She reminds me of an article that I once wrote on publicity:

In the Naughty Nineties when we all vainly imagined that immortality and lust had truly reached an all time high, the only thing lacking was "Publicity," The best families and aristocrats feared and shunned it, and I can recall seeing a little girl at a local fair receiving a sound shaking from her nurse who said, "Really, Miss Mary, if you go on like this, you'll get your name in the papers! Just think of that!"

Now there is a mad rush to "make the papers" and in any guise. Actors who are slipping hit other actors in night clubs— or get their faces slapped by their current girlfriends— use prohibited drugs, do a local jail sentence and depart on a well-paid personal appearance in the press.

The sleeping pill method is another angle, and any hysterical misunderstood grabs the "Pheno" bottle and takes just the right number to arrive on the front page and perhaps the movies. Pickets walking aimlessly in solemn circles opposite shops, perk up and grin at the sight of a flashbulb, and a "strike" that is not going so well is organized to produce a scrimmage or scuffle— a few beating, kicks and overturned cars, but always in full view of the camera boys. When they absent themselves, the whole thing goes back to a state of quiet boredom.

I once saw a motor accident, cops, ambulance, etc. compete. The two girls involved carefully applied lipstick and posed for the camera before stepping into the ambulance. Policemen will tell stories of how most criminals love publicity and while being dragged from the scene will shout to the cameramen, "What paper do you work for?"

There is no limit to what some people will do for a little limelight.

Chapter Five

The Kennedys
Those Barefoot Irish Peasants

It seems that many, many years ago, old Joe Kennedy gave Gloria Swanson the money to start her own production company which didn't do too well. Too, he set her up with an elegant apartment on Fifty-Sixth Street in New York, to which he had a private entrance. It seems to me the apartment was on the tenth floor. For years he gave her numerous pieces of jewelry— thousands and thousands of dollars worth. Mrs. Rose Kennedy knew of the relationship, but evidently she thought best to just ignore it.

Much, much later, I believe after Kennedy became ambassador, he asked Gloria to gather all the jewelry that he had given her and to go to Cartier's to have it reset in some unique settings. After taking it down to Cartier's— which was quite close— old Kennedy rushed back in and gathered the jewelry, saying that it must be insured first. So off to the insurance company they went. Leaving the jewelry there for appraisal, Gloria Swanson never saw the jewelry again. Now that lets you know what a Kennedy is like. Such a scoundrel!

Because of some large donation— one hundred thousand dollars, I believe— to pay Roosevelt's campaign expenses, old Kennedy was able to get named as the American Ambassador to Great Britain. Roosevelt asked him, "Why do you want to go to the Court of St. James?"

Old Joe said, "Because there hasn't been a Catholic Ambassador there since Henry the Eight and because I want my children to marry into the peerage."

You see, old Kennedy wanted his sons and daughters to go to Europe— in particular, England— in hopes that they might marry royalty— dukes or something. Pardon me, I have to laugh at that!

They have a nice custom over there when they hold court; it's a beautiful occasion. A grand ball to mark the ambassador's announcement with the Queen in attendance was given. And what a ball it was! The decorations and flowers were matched only by the magnificent attire of the people. The men wore velvet coats with diamond buckles at their knee breeches. Everywhere dress uniforms, Order of the Diamond Stickpin and the Order of Garter, were to be seen.

According to protocol, the new Ambassador attends in his new uniform. Instead, old Joe Kennedy insulted the Queen by wearing what appeared to be an American golfing outfit— a brown suit with a colored tie and brown shoes. The Lord Chamberlain stopped him at the door and told him that he would give him time to go back and change; but old Joe said, "I'm an American and I don't change for anyone. If they don't like my brown suit, I'll go home." The court gasped in astonishment when he entered.

The custom is for the Queen, who sits on a throne alongside the King, to have certain ambassadors brought up to her. She then holds out her *left* hand, they kiss it, and they begin the dancing by a slow ceremonial waltz once around the room with Her Majesty. But Old Joe comes up, grabs her *right* hand after she offered her left, telling her "wrong hand!"; pumps it, saying, "Howdy-do, I'm pleased to meet you"; and proceeded to dash her about the floor in a polka several times around the room. The Queen, always a lady first, tried to smile, but only a few moments later, told the new ambassador, "That is sufficient," and sat down.

Little wonder the people of England did not want the Kennedys in the Royal Circle. Old Kennedy seemed as crude and boorish as he was a scoundrel.

Later, when World War II began, old Kennedy decided to take his family back to New York. He walked into the "holy of holies"— Number 10 Downing Street— unannounced and told Churchill, "Hi!" Because he was so terrified at a bomb every four minutes during the Blitz— I was there— he, Mrs. Kennedy and the family fled on the plane after the first bomb. God fancy having to live that down! I always write music shops for the song that goes: *We won't go over till it's over, over there.* It was very popular here and was sung in the London music halls midst fits of laughter. The music and words are American— the Americans a brave people? Even Her Majesty and the Princess and all the Royal Family remained in London during the Blitz.

Old Wheelchair Kennedy, who called himself Ambassador to London, was kicked out by Churchill and he should have done it sooner. The mob had already put rubber baby pants on the door of the embassy because Kennedy was so terrified of the Blitz. I don't like Churchill and I never did. Such a mousey wife he had! The bribe to get the ambassadorship was nothing. Old Kennedy was the Bootleg King of the Prohibition Age. It's been said that he was in close contact with Al Capone, and since Capone's death, he inherited Capone's men.

The fire of hell isn't too hot for Old Kennedy. Have you ever heard of such a scoundrel!

Old Mr. Kennedy had a stroke. I did the correct thing and telegraphed my condolences. Three months later, I received an official reply from his New York office saying, "Your telegram received."

When Jack Kennedy started his Presidential campaign, he had a party arranged for him at one hundred dollars a plate. Upon my requesting it, my daughter-in-law offered me a ticket saying, "If you can find someone to let you sit at their table."

I declined, foreseeing the comments it would cause and the endless calls by the press asking "why?" So, I informed the press that I was ill with the flu. Later, a friend told me that there were three vacant places at Jack Kennedy's table. "What happened to you?" my friend asked me.

During the Presidential election, the *Times* of London called me up to say that they were told I was the Senior Lady in the British Colony in America. If so, why was I not at the many private and public dinners for Mr. Kennedy? I said I had no idea except that the Kennedy family is not too hot on etiquette or protocol.

One hour later, the same voice said, "I am terribly sorry; I checked. I did not know that you were bedridden!"

"For how long?" I asked.

Mrs. Pat Lawford had told them: "Years," he said, and hung up.

Oh, never would I have voted for Jack Kennedy, even if I had been an American citizen. Jack always had his mind down between his legs. No, I would have voted for Nixon. I like Nixon. I never spoke to him, but I think he was a good man. Jack was one of the family, but I think Nixon is so much more mature. And I would have voted for Reagan for governor. He's a fighter, I think. You can talk to a man— like the General— for just ten minutes and you realize that he's got control of the whole situation. This Vietnam thing would not have gone on all this long, long time. The General would have gone over there and he'd have said, "I want that bombed to hell today and I want them bombed to hell tomorrow. And I want this done and don't come back to tell me it can't be done, it is going to be!" You know— a dynamic, forceful man, full of push.

After the widely publicized Kennedy "Family Dinner," I was approached by columnists, newsmen and reporters asking for a guest list and other details. A young reporter found out that the Family Dinner was headed by Frank Sinatra and the young colored boy, Sammy Davis. This is *family?* Mrs. Joseph Kennedy arrived and no one mentioned it to me, though on previous occasions I had acted as chauffeur to her. This time I was ignored.

I don't know why Peter associates himself with that Rat Pack crowd. That dried-up piece of spaghetti— Sinatra— but I do like his singing— he's the villain of the piece. He loathes me and I must say the feeling is mutual. Not since Mickey Rooney and Van Johnson has Peter chosen such poor cronies. They dress alike; they drive cars alike; and they call each other these funny names like "Charley." I remember Peter and Pat hugging and kissing that nigger boy— Sammy Davis— and calling him "Chickie" or something like that. I may have embarrassed Peter with the Kennedys— I don't know how— but it seems Peter is proving an embarrassment to them as well. It's Sammy Davis— oh, it's no secret that he is the real embarrassment. He's always hanging around Peter and Pat— all these people in The Clan are the same.

Peter was not a drinker as long as he lived with the General and me— that was until he was thirty-two. The Kennedys seemed to have influenced his drinking. Always Patricia seemed to have a drink in her hand.

Remember when Jacqueline Kennedy went to France? DeGaulle winked at her and told her, "You could do very well here." You don't think that he was referring to French streetwalking, do you?

Certainly the clothes of Jacqueline Kennedy and Patricia Lawford do not reflect ladies of proper breeding. As the Montreal finishing school stated, "Mini-skirts are not befitting ladies and we do not accept the other kind!" You might know the Duchess of Windsor would wear such— you know that she is even older than the Duke? Certainly the Queen of England would never wear a mini-skirt. After all, she is a lady first and a queen second.

And that Lee Bouvier— you know, she married that divorced nobleman that every Englishman calls Prince *Who?*

The in-laws of Peter have said enough about, and I quote, "Peter's marriage being a disaster."

Mrs. Joe Kennedy told friends she "is sorry her family is allied with those awful Lawfords."

I am more than happy to have nothing to do with them in any way in the future, as sorry as I am about the grandchildren.

As the Senior Lady of the large British Colony— I believe, Lady Hardwicke, Sir Cedric Hardwicke's wife, used to be— in America, they, the Kennedys, found it difficult to "brush me under the rug!"

I have many friends in America and the climate is good to arthritis, which I have had since I was sixteen-years-old, and I don't want to leave... they'll never drive me out. Never!

I know that the Kennedys are not frightfully keen on me. Well, I was not too happy about Peter marrying into the Kennedy family, although I must say they've done well as a family. Only in "A-mer-i-cer"— as they say it— could barefoot Irish peasants have become the so-called "First Family." Surely when they call Jackie Kennedy "the First Lady," they are not equating her with the Queen, are they? Somewhere there is a book published that says something about "the only touch of aristocracy in the Kennedy family is Sir Sidney and Lady Lawford." Little wonder they are not keen on me.

Fancy the Kennedys being listed in Burke's Peerage.

Lawford, Liet. -Gen. Sir Sydney Turing Barlow, K.C.B. (1918), B.C. (1915) late Royal Fus.: Asst. Cmdt. School of Mounted Infantry 1907-10; Commandant 1912-13; Comm. Essex Brigade 1913-14, and Brig.-Gen. comdg. 22nd Inf. Brig. B.E.F. 1914; 41st Div. 1915-20; served in S. African War 1901-2 (Queen's Medal with three clasps, brevet), and in Great War (despatches seven times); has 4th class Order of St. Vladimir of Russia; Crois de Guerre of France and Belgium, and is Commander Order of St. Maurice and St. Lazarus of Italy, Legion of Honour and Order of Leopold of Belgium; b. 16 Nov. 1865; son of late Thomas Acland Lawford, of Kinellan, Wimbledon Common; m. 1st 20 May 1914, Muriel (who obtained a divorce 1924 and d. 9 Aug. 1936), dau. of Sir Hartley Williams; and 2ndly, 1924, May Sommerville, dau. of Col. F.W. Bunny, Roy. Berks. Regt. Address— Army and Navy, Royal Automobile and Ravelagh Clubs.

A man tried to "give" me a picture of a man coming down the hall of a Beverly Hills call-house. It was worth nothing to me. Why did I want it? Why should I pay money for a picture of my daughter-in-law's brother? It meant nothing to me.

However, it did mean something to old Joe Kennedy. After he had **procured** the picture of Jack Kennedy, he left it lying on the bed. When later, Jackie Kennedy saw the picture lying on the bed, she became greatly upset and cried, "I won't stay with him; I refuse to

remain with him anymore!"

Whereupon old Joe Kennedy offered his daughter-in-law a check. The check was for one million dollars! The payoff: to remain married to Jack. Jackie Kennedy was a clever girl; such a good businesswoman. She said, "Make it tax free and it's a deal."

Yes, there was quite a ruckus about Peter's landing his helicopter on the beach. So many people on the beach would rush up and go "ooh" and "aah." Often the crowds would rush forward in hopes of seeing President Kennedy. After Jack Kennedy's death, orders were issued for Peter's bright yellow helicopter to stop landing on the beach.

Bobby Kennedy was often a guest at Peter and Patricia's beach house. In fact, it seems to me that Bobby was at Peter's house at the time of Marilyn Monroe's death. I can't help but recall that time out at Peter's house when Bobby, grown and already married, sat with a small table between his legs in the den and, armed with knife and fork, kept screaming loudly like a child: "I want my lunch! I want my lunch! I want my lunch!"

I bet that you did not know that Jack Kennedy kept two airplane hostesses out there. He had met them when he was traveling across country as Senator. One girl lived in the Venice community, I believe, and the other inside Santa Monica. You didn't know, did you? I liked Jack, but his mind was always on his cock.

Marilyn Monroe seemed such a lovely girl. I once asked Peter why he did not invite her to some of our parties. He said, "I don't think she is *your* cup of tea, Mother." But he and Pat saw her often.

The night that Marilyn died, I called Peter out at the Santa Monica beach house. The telephone lines were very busy, but I finally got through. "I've been robbed!" I exclaimed to Peter, who could have cared less about my dwindling jewel and silver collection. In the background I thought I heard that awful Boston accent of Bobby Kennedy. "Later" was Peter's one word solution to my concern over the third break-in and burglary. Then he hung up.

The next day when I heard about Marilyn's last phone call to Peter,

I realized that my call to Peter the previous night— about eight o'clock— was near the same time. Peter told me that Marilyn ended their telephone call with the words, "Say goodbye to Pat, say goodbye to Jack (JFK), and say goodbye to yourself, because you're a nice guy, Charley." She just had to call Peter by that atrocious nickname "Charley". I heard that he acquired it from the Rat Pack because his constant cigarette cough reminded them of the character Charley the Seal. Anyway, I think it's an awful nickname!

I felt Peter was awfully mean to Marilyn. After all, on the evening that she died she had called him on the telephone and had said goodbye to everyone there at his beach house. Then she dropped the telephone as a result of her loss of consciousness. Peter had run to her rescue before (just as he had with Judy Garland) when she pleaded over the phone for him to come over. However, this time was different because she said "goodbye". "Goodbye" sounded final.

"How could you be so unfeeling when that lovely girl's life was at stake?" I asked Peter when I finally managed to get through to him. Peter reluctantly told me that he asked his manager Milton Ebbins to go with him over to Marilyn's house. Peter said that his first impulse was to call doctors and order an ambulance.

"You can't go over to Marilyn's house!" exclaimed Milt Ebbins. "You're the brother-in-law of the President of the United States. Your wife is away in Hyannis Port. The publicity would be disastrous if it were discovered. I'll call her lawyer Mickey Rudin or her doctor, and they will go to see about her."

"Yes, but Peter," I insisted, "you are the one that she turned to; you are the one who talked to her. You are the one who should have gone to help her. If you had gone, perhaps she would have been alive today."

By this time Peter was more than a bit agitated with me. Still, he explained that both Milton Ebbins and Mickey Rudin called him and assured him that Marilyn was all right so that finally Peter gave up the idea of going to Marilyn's house.

It all smells of fish to me. There is something fishy about the relationship of her physician Dr. Hyman Engelberg and her lawyer Mickey Rudin and his brother-in-law, her psychiatrist Dr. Ralph Greenson and her psychiatric nurse-turned housekeeper Mrs. Eunice Murray. And I wonder about her press agent-friend Pat Newcomb, who joined the Kennedys' staff immediately upon Marilyn's death.

It was the next morning that I heard that she was dead. Reports said the body was found at 3:40 a.m., but a reader of any well-written English mystery could figure out a before-midnight death by rigor mortis. That Jap coroner, Nuguchi, first said Marilyn had twenty-three different kinds of poisons in her, didn't he? Then, he said her stomach was clean as a whistle. Why didn't he ever say anything about the fresh injection in her armpit?

I knew that Marilyn was seeing Jack Kennedy. I also knew that Marilyn was seeing Bobby Kennedy. They often used Pat and Peter's beach house for their dalliances with Marilyn and airplane hostesses and movie starlets and only God knows who else! But what do you expect from the sons of Joe Kennedy? Old Joe paraded his women friends in front of his children and even had those women seated at his dinner table in the presence of his entire family. All the while Rose Kennedy lowered her eyes, played with her Irish linen handkerchief, and rushed to the next Mass. You know, she got God's "middleman", Pope Pius XII, to make her a "Papal Countess" for a two and one-half million dollar donation, and now she must be trying to earn stripes so she can become a "Papal Queen." One thing for certain, those Kennedys haven't the faintest idea what the *discretion* means. It is like I've said before, I like Jack Kennedy, but I find it difficult to place my complete trust in a President of the United States who always has his mind on his cock!

When I was talking to Peter about Marilyn's death, I did not mention to him that I knew his bright yellow helicopter was not parked by the beach house. Instead, a dark colored helicopter, like the Kennedy boys used to rent, had been parked at Peter's house. I did not say a word about having heard Bobby's voice in the background of the telephone call. I was totally mum about the neighbor who saw Bobby Kennedy going into Marilyn's house the afternoon of her death. Yet I could not remain totally quiet in speaking to my son so I slobberingly fawned on and on about the frontpage newspaper photograph of smiling Bobby Kennedy— taken of him in San Francisco supposedly about the same time of Marilyn's death the night before.

If we had not been talking on the telephone, I would have given Peter one of my "fisheyes"— like this. When I would lower my right eye into a quivering stare, Peter knew that the "fish eye" translated to "I don't believe a word that you tell me." Ever since his friendship days with Mickey Rooney and Van Johnson, Peter had mastered the art of lying. But a mother innately knows when her child "is telling the whole truth, and nothing but the truth, so help you God." Another feature of Peter's complex personality was the extreme influence on him by those closest to him. I used to be concerned about his "loyal servant" attitude toward bosom buddy Frank Sinatra. If Sinatra and his questionable cronies asked Peter to do something for them in the name of friendship, he would do it whether it was right or wrong. Don't you think that alcohol and drugs poisoned Peter's judgment? This same situation existed with the Kennedys. Peter was so enamoured of the so-called Kennedy charisma that if Jack or Bobby asked him to, he would have done anything—legal or illegal. So it is with Marilyn's death—Peter had a part in the cover-up. I wonder if all of the mystery will ever be solved?

I do believe that ball player, Joe DiMaggio, still loves her. Every time I visit that cemetery, he has sent her more flowers. You know, the story almost had a happy ending— DiMaggio flew to Los Angeles on August 5, 1962, to remarry Marilyn Monroe. Instead, he buried her.

Chapter Six

Do You Know The Duchess?

How dare you! The Duchess— that whore! It doesn't make any difference that all that was back in 1936—she was a prostitute. Several of the naval officers had slept with her. One officer who had slept with her said she was quite good, but not *that* good!

The Duke of Windsor was such a miserable child; almost no one could tolerate him. Even as early as nine, he was a budding alcoholic. After every party, he would drink all the remainders in the glasses— just like Peter did. Soon after this age, he began to drink heavily— a bottle of bourbon in the morning. He was— you know— by twelve o'clock noon, he was "hic." Why, he often wet his pants because he was so drunk. Remember, I told you the story of how the General had to order him down from his polo pony, he was so drunk.

Once I was at a party with the Duke— he was the young prince then. Being a small affair and being customary, I was expected to dance with the drunken heir to the throne. Now Fruity Metcalf was his aide and I've known Fruity ever since he was that high. I said to Fruity, "I'm not going to dance with him. Get him out of the room before he starts vomiting, you ass!"

"Is she going to dance with me?" The Duke asked Fruity. And as he did, a gold cigarette case that would choke a horse— about that long— fell out of his shirt. If he sent me to The Tower, I would never dance with him!

"Get him the hell out of here," I said once again to Fruity, "before he starts vomiting, you ass."

So Fruity, leading him toward the door, said, "Sirrah, I think perhaps we should go." As they left, I overheard the Duke say, "She won't dance with me?" and Fruity said, "She won't dance with anybody."

Like I said, the Duke had numerous mistresses, but the General told me that he drank so much that he was notoriously bad in bed. It sounds like he might have been just right for *me* in that way. Anyway, he met this Wallis Simpson from America at a party. The English say it, but I don't know if it's true, that her first words to him were, "Would you like a drink?" Yes, the Duke had found a drinking buddy. A Yank at that and even a twice divorced one. Later, they were together at Epson where their cars remained out front for three days. All of London was abuzz.

Wallis Simpson, coming from a common Baltimore boarding house, was smart. Her price was evidently a ring on her finger, and that drunken Duke paid it. Of course, *she* had a reputation of being quite good in bed. I'm sure the Duke was even drunk when he married her. You know they say the duchess' mother maintained the same boarding house near Baltimore where Wallis waited tables. I can just see the old lady with her tin cup showing tourists and curiosity-seekers the duchess' bedroom and the bath. Ha!

I told you the story of the Duchess of Windsor and how she tried to take jewels from the Royal Collection. What happened was, she was left alone in the home in England while the Duke, upon announcing his abdication, went over to stay with old Baron Eugene Rothschild, an old Jew, who lived in France. And the Duke was in kind of a shock so Rothschild said he could come over. The Duke cost Rothschild four hundred dollars a day in telephone calls; he telephoned all over the world— busy, busy, busy— and he didn't pay a cent!

Anyway, to make a long story short— while the Duchess was left there in England, she called the King's aide. She told him she wanted to go over and for him to show her Queen Alexandra's jewels— she had the finest collection of jewels in the world. And so the Duchess thought because the Duke is over there, she might just as well get things over so she had the aide show her the jewels and tried them on to see how Queen Anne had worn them, and the Duchess never gave them back. She had "forgot" to give them back. She said to her maid to put them in her bag and take it down to her cabin. So she got on the naval ketch and they got half-way across. They— the British— had the swiftest boats in the world. They could outdo any ocean liner, any regular ferry boat, but not the naval boats.

The Keeper of the Royal Jewels— my father used to have his office right near there and I used to go past the great big rooms filled with all these wonderful diamonds and wonderful pearls; the Cullinan diamond was about *that* big, and I used to keep my hat boxes in my father's office so that's how I used to go right past the Royal Jewels....I used to buy and wear hats in those days— anyway, he discovered the things gone.

"My God," the Keeper of the Royal Jewels said, "she's taken Queen Anne's diamonds and jewels with her— thousands and thousands and thousands of dollars of jewels with her!"

Scotland Yard got its boat and "shhhhhhhh". It stood up like that; here's their cutter boats and here's the naval ketch. "Stop in the name of the law,"the police shouted. The Captain, two policeman and the Scotland Yard people went on board where they had policed the Duchess' cabin day and night. They didn't say to her, 'Pull over, sister." Ha! They said, "Madam, kindly hand over the jewels of Queen Alexandra's."

"But they are mine," the Duchess protested. "They were given to me by my fiance!" (She mispronounced the French word.)

"We know that would be quite all right," they said to her, "but they cannot be yours; they are listed in the Queen's Royal Jewels."

"Oh, no, no, that's a lot of rot!"she retorted.

So the Scotland Yard people said, "Boys, let's get the engine started," and she, upon hearing the engines, asked, "What's that?"

"Well, we're going back to London" was the answer.

"I don't know what to do," she whined. "My poor home has been ruined. Every pane of glass has been broken. The mob will give the King a threat!"

"It is quite simple," they told her. "You deliver us the jewels, we'll take them back; we'll give you a receipt for them; and then they can be put back in the Royal Collection. Then you can be on your way."

So she didn't get them. No, she didn't get to keep *any* of them.

I shall never forget the time when the General and I were dining in London when the Duke and Mrs. Simpson entered. Every Englishman— almost the whole of the people eating— got up from their seats and walked out of the restaurant. Why, of course, *I* walked out!

Queen Mary, I think, did wrong by the Duchess. She was not so strong as Queen Elizabeth. Elizabeth has merely said, "How do you do" to her all these years. I would never speak to him. I never went near him after his marriage. However, Peter saw them not so long ago in Palm Beach.

When the General and I were living in Nassau, the General received a letter from the War Office in London that stated that he must leave his card at the Governor's House, the residence of the Duke and Duchess of Windsor, there in Nassau.

Surely, I thought, the General would not follow such a request. But if he did not— I finally asked the General:

"What can happen?"

"I am going out there to do what I was told to do," he said. "I've always done what was right and I'm going to do it now."

So we went there to the Governor's House and fortunately they were away from Nassau— she was probably away having her face lifted. The man, a contemporary of the General, who was there, said to me:

"Do you want to see a view of the worst taste in the world?"

"What do you mean?" I asked.

"Come with me," was his reply.

So he took me into the drawing room— I had been there very often, not with them, but with the previous governor. Here was this awful room— awful all over. She had gone and bought up what looked like all the Union Jacks in the world! And she had made then into curtains; she had made covers for the foot-stools; she had made covers for the couches of the Union Jack. The flag of the British Empire! Never shall I forget the drawing room decorated with Union Jacks. I had to laugh at the Duchess' tastelessness.

The Duchess of Windsor and I had the same hairdresser in Monte Carlo, so I heard all the things she said. She said one day, "I don't want to have my hair done unless there are a lot of people here." So the hairdresser used to make a face at me and give me a knowing look.

I've often heard that she paid $100,000 to be named on the the Ten Best-Dressed Women list.

Oh, the Duchess was clever in selling all those awful pictures. Thank goodness for the Duchess gathering all of those unprinted pictures and selling them to *Life* and *Look* magazines. This money enabled them to live rather comfortably.

Everyone has the mistaken idea that royalty has wealth. It just is not true if you are inside the court circle and know the true story. For example, you just assumed that the Duke of Windsor had money. No, even with all his land titles, the Duke did not actually have money in hand. The Crown gave him nothing upon his abdication. Luckily, the Duke had a four hundred acre farm in Canada off which he received $250 a month. Not much for royalty!

Pierre Cartier told me that he loaned the Duke more than a hundred thousand dollars. Later I went to Australia on the same ship as Cartier — Pierre Cartier. You know the Duchess owes her own jewels to Pierre. Pierre said that they come into one of his shops and buy everything that they pick out — and none of them are paid for! The Duke owed Pierre 3 0 0, 0 0 0 .0 0 dollars. I said, "Pierre, you'll never get a dime; I know that type."

He said that he never expected to be repaid. He said that the Duke owed an awful lot of money and that eventually the Crown would pay for it upon his death.

Of course I know the Duchess — the Duchess de Salverte! Actually, she preferred "Comtesse Jeanne de Salverte." You do know Jan, don't you? She was the countess who married the Count de Salverte

— in Paris today there is a street named Rue Salverte. Oh, he had millions which he had made in the stock market. What a marvelous wedding they had! I was too young to attend, but I remember hearing of all the white horses and white gardenias. Yes, I had those at my wedding,too — six white horses. After the wedding, Jan found that the Duke had a place down at *Pigalle* Street or one of those dark alleys where he kept his mistress. She followed him there one night; then returned home to wait for him. She pounced upon him with such force that he was battered black and blue. The battle and the injuries were glorified in the newspapers, but they did not begin to match the Count's battered ego. Jan had gotten her revenge.

I dearly love Jan and we were the best of friends. She was not a pretty woman. It seemed as if she were six foot three inches tall. Nevertheless, she had many beaux. Always the men gathered about her. She was an excellent shot. She could shoot anything on land, under water or in the air. What a horsewoman!

And completely crazy about golf. Often she and the General would spend the day at Sunningdale. Once while she was at Sardinia for open singles, one of her many admirers followed her, but to no avail. He knew that we were the best of friends.

He took me to Cartier's in Paris and showed me an extraordinary diamond bracelet about three and one-half inches wide saying that it was mine if I could convince Jan to marry him. I told him that as a countess, she had her own wealth and had obtained some more property through marriage to the duke. Then I asked if he could afford Jan; he assured me that he had millions — possibly billions through his underwater gold mines.

However, the handsome Duke d'Orleans, pretender to the French throne, claimed Jan's heart. It seemed to make no difference with him that she was considerably older and that she wore her hair short and combed straight back from her unevenly-featured face. Soon they became inseparable. Together at every ball, together at every party, together in every country on a safari. They never married, but were constant companions until his death. Knowing that they maintained separate houses, I still questioned Jan.

"Even though you don't live together as man and wife, I'm sure you are guilty of adultery."

"Oh no," she said, "there is a difference; although we sleep together, it is not adultery. You see, neither one of us is married."

You know, my dear friend Jan, the Countesse de Salverte, almost married a Negro? No, no, not her first husband — that was the Duke. Then she fell in love with the Duke of Orleans. I once asked her, "How do you keep the wolf at bay?"

She quickly retorted, "I don't."

Never had I heard of "the such" — as my nigger maid used tosay. She and d'Orleans were together for years, but never married. The Negro, Segrid Asked, was a rajah from India and very immensely wealthy. He's the one who begged me to marry him.

Sex was very casual with Jan — she said it was like washing and drying your hands.

Later, when Jan retired from public life, after the death of the Duke d'Orleans, she and the Queen of Spain went to Switzerland. They invited me to join them there to live. I just had one thing to say: One old bag is bad enough; two old bags are worse; but three old bags are ridiculous!

Yes, I know the Duchess Youcheff. 'Lizabeth the Leech is what I call her. Oh, the Duchess Slav Youcheff — such a sot! I met her at a party here in Los Angeles and could never get rid of her. She clamped on like a parasite.

I remember one morning about eleven o'clock, Slav — her husband, the Duke — called me and said, "Oh, May, help me!"

I dressed properly and drove over only to find they had been fighting. There lay the Duchess on the floor babbling like an idiot. Well, the only thing to do was to commit her to the psycho ward. Of course, Slav couldn't stand to see her there; but perhaps there they could "dry her out" from alcohol. How she did gulp down Cointreau! Finally, her brother in Fullerton, California, had her released and she stayed with him.

Next she and Slav went to Cincinnati to visit a sister. Finally, she wound up in Miami, Florida. Slav, or "Duke" as she called him, much to everyone's amusement, saw a man in Budapest with long, luxuriant hair all the way to his waist. When he asked the man about it, the man told him of a herb salve. Since then, he and the Duchess have tried to peddle the stuff. You know the old saying: There's a sucker born every day! I think that Slav died in 1954. At least he wouldn't have to live through anymore of her drunken spells in which she would chase him with a butcher knife.

Anyway, the Duchess came to visit me a few years ago. She was so drunk that she checked into both the Hilton downtown and the big one out on Wilshire going toward Santa Monica. She actually forgot which hotel she was registered in and had to pay both. She is very "taken" with the idea of royalty and titles as shown by calling Slav "Duke" in front of friends. She wants to be referred to as "the Duchess" or "Her Highness." Ha, Her Highness the Sot!

Oh, my God, I received a letter from the Duchess Youcheff today. She wants to visit me out here. Please inform her that my arthritis is bothering me so I cannot have guests at the present time. Listen to her letter:

Dearest May:
   I miss you so very much. We had such fun together! And Slave was devoted to you — he loved stopping off at your home for real English tea.
   How I wish I could come out to see you. I have $150.00 a month to live on as a consultant's fee until sales begin the latter part of November and my royalty has to be a minimum of $1000 a month for my people to keep the distributorship of McLarans Hair Dressing. I am to be on the "Today Show" as soon as we get under way. I am to receive fifty cents for a two-ounce jar of McLarans which will sell for $7.50 or $10,00 — not yet decided upon. I believe anyone will tell you that's about the very highest royalty ever paid in the cosmetic business — then there is fifty cents for a four-ounce jar of McLarans Hair Dressing! *And* for a lady!
   Oh, May, it has been dreadful without Slav. I was left so little, if at all, prepared to go into the business world. It was a whole new world— new and difficult people — new and different everything!
   ... I hate living alone — I hope to marry again — but there is no one here of our religion, if you know what I mean. Then, too, I have had nothing on my mind but to get my business over and get back to you and my world.

Poor Duchess! Elizabeth — that's her given name — Elizabeth is a good example of so-called royalty in America. She has faced her share of problems — marital difficulties, financial straits and a terrible drinking problem. Now it seems she want to pick up the pieces. Poor dear! The letter continues:

I have not written any friend whomsoever — nor sent Christmas cards since 1966 — *excepting you,* May, I do not know if I have any friends left. Beginning today, with you, I shall write two or three letters a day, explain and ask forgiveness and understanding!

Copy the enclosed letter in your own words and send to me at once.

For prestige, address my letter air-mail European Style!

Her Highness, Duchess Youcheff
6578 S.W. 37th Street
Miami, Florida 33155

Elizabeth darling:

I am so happy for you — How dreadful this must have been for you alone!

Come to me and be my houseguest for a week — to recuperate (clear you mind, as well as anyone could be physically) — we will shop and have lunch, etc., like we always did. Time passes — things change — Darling Slav won't be here to have tea with us — and pick you up — neither will Pat and Peter be here — nor the children — but come any time and we'lll have fun and I'll get you back in your own world!

Love — May

Chapter Seven

Who's Who In My Life

Once many years ago Mrs. Frank Sinatra asked about Peter's English valet. She said that Frankie was in bad need of a manservant to handle his personal wardrobe. After discussing it with Peter, I told her that Peter agreed to lend Frank his valet. After only a short while on his first day there, the valet told Mrs. Sinatra that he had finished pressing all that he could find — one business suit and one tuxedo plus a couple of pairs of slacks. "Where is the rest?" he asked. To which she replied, "That is all he has." The valet then told her that he couldn't finish Peter's pressing in a whole day. She then assured him she would have more work for him next time. The next time it was the same situation — the pressing of the same meager wardrobe. When the valet asked about more, she handed him a pail of sudsy water and a sponge, and told him to wash the windows. Appalled, the valet said, "A gentleman's gentleman does not wash windows!"

One evening we were invited to dinner at Frank Sinatra's Toluca Lake home. Oh, how lovely it was. The General and I drove in our car; Peter, who was working on a picture, was to drive his own car. We, the General and I, arrived first and Sinatra asked where Peter was. I said, "Peter? That *schmuck!*" Frank doubled up in howls of uncontrollable laughter. This went on for minutes. Even the General was greatly amused. When Peter arrived, Frank told him what I had called him, and they all huddled in whispers and laughed and laughed. To this day I don't know what the word "schmuck" really means!

After the Sinatra incident, Peter told me never to use the word again. I agreed not to use "schmuck" if he would not use "shit."

Several years ago during the Bel Air fire I worked in the animal food and grain shelter. The Taylor home — Liz's father, Francis, was an art dealer — was on a huge flat area on top of Bel Air equipped with four gardeners to keep the grounds. Elizabeth what-was-her-name then? Let's see, she was married to that Hilton boy for about a week, wasn't she? Then she married that charming Englishman, Michael Wilding. He was so nice. Then Todd and the plane crash. Why did she every marry that Fisher boy? Oh, did you know that Burton was a miner back in Wales? Anyway, Elizabeth — she always looked so beautiful at my parties — never paid for the two hundred dollars worth of grain that she bought from the animal shelter. Upon hearing that Liz had not paid the bill, Peter told me to stop bothering her and he paid for it himself.

I remember once when Jan de Salverte lost her pearls. Ah, such lovely cultured pearls given to her family by a dear friend, Marie Antoinette. I too had some Marie Antoinette pearls, but they were stolen. We searched high and low for Jan's pearls, but to no avail. When I went in and told the General of her loss, he put down *The Times* of London and exclaimed, "What a newspaper story this will be!" Then he had an idea: Send all of Jan's golfing shoes to him. Jan treasured her golfing shoes so much that she refused to let anyone clean them but herself. The General, remembering that Jan had the pearls on earlier when they were golfing, examined the shoes carefully.

Sure enough, there were the missing pearls in the toe of one of the shoes.

Then there was my friend Ward Price, the war correspondent. I can remember when we were staying in the same hotel once. Peter had gone to tell him what time dinner was to be. Right there in the hall he put his arms around Peter and pulled him toward him as if to kiss him on the lips. Peter resisted him saying later that "he thinks I'm something I'm not." Even though he did run on two currents — A.C. and D.C. I couldn't help but like him. After the General's death, he even asked me to marry him saying it would be advantageous for both of us.

When we were living in Hawaii, we often saw Howard Hughes. In fact, he and the General got on very well. In particular I remember a dinner at which I was seated next to him. What a horrible smell! Never had I smelled a man like him. I almost blurted out something about the stench when the General's eyes met mine and he lowered his eyes to Hughes' canvas shoes. Later the General explained that the billionaire apparently had a foot disease that caused the awful foot odor. I can never hear the name of Howard Hughes without holding my nose.

Mrs. Henry Ford — the first one, I mean — was such a dreadful snob. I only met her once and that was once too many. I'm sure that she would never have spoken to me if I had not had this handle attached to my name.

One time at the Sporting Club in Monte Carlo, Marlene Dietrich came up the stairs in trousers. Of course, she wasn't admitted. I remember when she had too much to drink and was telling all the Russian escorts how she had been a dishwasher in Germany. The maitre d's comment on Dietrich's trousers: "Lady Lawford, we shall telephone you as to whether to return next season."

Such a yacht! That Aristotle Onassis has such a tremendous boat. So often I saw it in Monte Carlo. Onassis would see me in the casino and say, "Why don't you ever play at my table?" or "When are going to visit me on my boat?" I would have eaten in the servant's hall first!

The old Kaiser once said to me, "Keep a wife barefoot, pregnant, and home in the kitchen" — I'm sure that it wasn't original with him. He was quite old when we had dinner together at Monte Carlo.

One evening there came into the casino such an extraordinarily beautiful woman. I commented on her gown, "That isn't an ordinary Christian Dior gown; that is a special-made gown just for her." I sent a waiter to ask who the gorgeous creature was, but before he returned, the lady had gone over next to the Kaiser. She was his wife!

The gown was black velvet — very low in the front — she was quite heavy up there and very tight in the skirt. It had slits of pink satin which showed when she walked. Her shoes were black velvet with pink enamel heels. A long evening cape of black velvet with pink satin lining was topped with a huge high collar of pink fox. Her earings and necklace were alternate strands of pink and black pearls. Her elbow high bracelets were just like the ones of London whores. *Service stripes* we called them!

For many years I have known Princess Stephanie Hohenhole — of the Austrian royalty. You know her husband was killed by the Reds — the Communists — but I don't think she cared much about him. Stephanie was very close to Hitler. Rumor had it that she was his girlfriend, but whatever — people could always get to Hitler through her.

One day she called me over the telephone crying that her mother had been hit by a Bekins van. I jumped in my car and rushed to where they lived — near Blum's in Beverly Hills. There I found the old lady still lying there in the street. I shouted, "Why don't you move her? Have you called a doctor?" No, they had not. Finally, I convinced them to take her to St. John's Hospital in Santa Monica. That next day   I called Stephanie to ask about her mother: the old lady had been dead almost twenty-four hours.

The old lady, Baroness Ludmilla Szepessy, had lived through a forced imprisonment in an asylum. Her daughter, Princess Stephanie Hohenlohe, who served as an U. S. envoy under Presidents Kennedy, Johnson, and Nixon, was placed in a Texas internment camp. Even her darling grandson, Prince Franzi Hohenlohe, who served in the U.S. Army, U.S. Navy, and the United Nations, was locked up too. J. Edgar Hoover of the F.B.I. is as much a scoundrel as old Joe Kennedy, don't you think?

Another time Louis B. Mayer asked me about Peter's peculiar

acquaintances. I said, "What are you trying to say — that my son is a homosexual? What's wrong? Did you ask him and he turned you down?" He looked at me in both disgust and amazement. He said, using his nickname for me, "I wouldn't take comments like that from anyone but 'The Thoroughbred Mare'!"

I am sure that Louis B. Mayer was referring to Peter's friendship with Van Johnson. At this time Van and Keenan Wynn were living together. Keenan was married to Evie. Then one day I came home to our drawing room in which Evie sat with Van (to whom she was now married), Keenan Wynn, Peter, and the General. Evie and Van had told Keenan that he could have the baby after much discussion, I stormed out of the room saying, "I don't give a damn who gets the baby — just shut it up!"

Whereupon I gave orders to our servants never to allow Van or Evie in our drawing room again: "We simply are not home to *them* in the future !" Peter was quite upset at me for storming out and refusing them further admittance. I said, "I don't want homosexuals in our drawing room. If you want them here, then notify me and I will leave while they are here." I'm glad the General died; he could never enjoy the company and conversation of these "types."

One evening I went into the General and announced that Emmuska Orczy, the author of *Scarlet Pimpernel* wanted us to dinner with her star, Merle Oberon. The General laughed, "Good old port in any storm!" He said that in Bombay all the servicemen who slept with her called her that. I said that Merle must be good in bed — at least, better than me. To which the General retorted, "That wouldn't be hard!"

At a party one evening —it must have been in the early forties— were the three Gabor girls and their mother straight from Hungary. At the time they were staying in a three-dollar-a-night motel. Mama Jolie Gabor went to the impresario who was handling Peter at the time and told him she wanted a rich husband for one of her daughters who had left her diplomat husband and their father back in Hungary. I suppose that was Zsa Zsa who later married Conrad Hilton. I understand when the marriage ended, he settled two million on the child, Francesca, that he so badly had wanted.

Jolie Gabor was introduced to me as being of French extract so I began talking to her in French, but she quickly interrupted me saying she was Hungarian. Remember when they had those awful fires in Bel Air? Zsa Zsa went on television saying, "My paintings, my valuable paintings were all burned!" However, some man had put them in a van and had saved them.

On a panel show one evening I was to meet Pamela Mason. Of course, I remember her before James Mason entered her life — back when she lived with Kellino without being married to him. One good thing I must say for her: She does love cats! We were to be introduced, but she, still in her dressing room applying make-up, indicated that she did not wish to meet me. That conniving bitch, I can't understand why!

Anyway, on the panel show later she was asked what she would teach her children about God. She said, "Nothing." She preferred that they grow up naturally and adopt their own ideas.

Of course, I refuted this idea. I said that very early I taught Peter to pray "Now lay me down to sleep" — in fact, I still pray this prayer myself. I taught him to believe in God, that God was good, and that God would forgive any sins — large or small. I think that it is very important to give a child the proper religious foundation. But obviously Pamela Mason didn't.

My father was in charge of command on Malta — the island on which my mother died. My mother often had dinner for Winston Churchill. One evening she was having dinner with him on the Admiral's yacht. When they came up from dinner, the men were still dancing. Sir Winston exclaimed, "Haven't they got any homes?" My mother who loves the servicemen really had a falling out with the statesman over this.

Even though my father made us promise never to utter the name of Winston Churchill after the statesman and my mother crossed swords, I did know the Churchill family quite well. But oh, that drunken Sarah Churchill! Everyone knew she was a drunk. I felt sorry for Lady Churchill — such an ugly dear. You know, her family and mine cross about eight hundred and twenty years back. I believe it was the same lineage as Queen Anne.

Anyway, Sarah Churchill was not only a drunk, but she was quite sexy too. Remember the time she was arrested in a bar for public drunkenness? Two policemen hauled her to a squad car. As one policeman pushed her into the back seat, she reached for his pants zipper and jerked it down. She said, ":Now let's see what kind of man you are!"

Sarah Churchill was making a picture — something about "Marriage" in the title — with Peter. Peter called her "that bitch" and threatened to go to Louis B. Mayer about her. One night Peter suggested I invite her for tea so I made the invitation for the next day at four o'clock. About seven the next evening Sarah and her present husband appeared in our drawing room. I said, "The invitation was for tea at four o'clock this afternoon; not seven o'clock for dinner. I'm sorry that we are not prepared to serve you. Give my best to your father." Her husband — a dear boy who I really liked — stood in agreement with me nodding sheepishly. I'm sure that she thought I was a bitch. You know, lots of women call me a bitch and I guess I am.

Did you ever hear of Bugsy Siegal? He was in with all the gangster set and also in with what Beverly Hills calls society. Often I was at parties with him. And that woman — Virginia Hill was her name — was quite open about sleeping with him. Some women would say "slept with." but she was the kind who bragged about "laying with Siegal." I believe that story that she told the House-Un—American Activities on live television that she was "the best goddamn lay on the West Coast." The General made me mad one evening as we were returning home from one of her parties. He said about Miss Hill, "She'll never have to worry about starvation," The General said that Virginia Hill was always surrounded by men at parties. I retorted that *I* was too; he said, "Yes, but not for the same reason.

On another evening we were at a Beverly Hills home — hers, I think — anyway, it was raining something frightful. So the General and I decided to wait before leaving. I sat down at the oppostie end of the sofa from Bugsy and we looked out the window at the rain. Finally, when the rain ceased, the General, and I returned home. Not long after, Mickey Cohen, a friend of the General, called the General and told him that Bugsy had been murdered. In fact, he was shot at the end of the same sofa where I had sat that recent evening.

I remember Wendy Barrie, the English actress, whose mother once asked me, "Did you call my daughter a whore?" "No," I said, "but is she?"

I once heard a story about Wendy Barrie — I don't know if it is true. Heaven help us if it is the truth. It seems that a big black nigger burglar broke into Miss Barrie's house not far from here. He **threatened** her life and demanded her jewels and furs which she quickly gave to him. Just as he was **leaving**, he noticed a diamond pendant around her neck, and he grabbed for it. "Oh no, please don't take it!" she begged. It was supposedly a gift to her from a gangster boyfriend —I think it was Bugsy Siegal — and she attached much sentimental value to it. "Take anything but it," she pleaded to which he raised an eyebrow, and asked, "Anything?" After leading her to the bedroom, the burglar left later without taking the furs and jewels. Wendy Barrie's neighbors reported seeing a big black man enter and leave the house by the back door on many occasions afterwards. Oh, can you imagine!

Oh, Sharman Douglas, Ambassador Douglas' daughter, used to write every day to Peter — six thick letters every day. Registered. She would write: "Dear Peter, I want to tell you that your room is ready for you and has fresh flowers in it and we're so looking forward to your return.

One day I went to a party at Valerie Nelson's home. Valerie- he's dead now— resided in New York and he had a beautiful home in Bel Air. I came up the stairs— they had two levels— the drawing room was on the other level. Anyway, as I came up the stairs, I saw a man, the editor of the— what is that paper that is written about Hollywood and the stage, Variety?— I saw that man standing like *that* with his arms rather still and going "hic! hic!" Drunk as an owl. So I looked at him and he said, "This is Miss Douglas." And I said, "Thank you

so much. I don't want any part of it." And as I went away, he dragged
her over and gave her to the attendant who would call her a coach.
Sharman Douglas was so drunk she was dragging her feet like *that!*

The Aga Khan's son, Aly, visited in one of the lower countries
inhabited mainly by Negroes. While there he picked up a habit that
led him to sexual success. When he returned to his harem of thirteen
and fourteen-year-old girls, he practiced this concept of "multiple
climax." You know I don't really quite understand it; it is something
men do only. Thank heavens the General only asked for "one
happening." When Aly wed that Tijuana dancer— oh, what was her
name?— Rita Cansino— no, *Hayworth*. I'm sure his sex appeal had
something to do with it. He was a great favorite among ladies.

The Riad Ghalis— oh, do I remember them! She is the daughter of
the Egyptian King Farouk. What a fat belly that man had. He used to
ask me to just stand still and let him look at me. The old geyser
would undress me mentally. You know I wasn't so bad looking in
those days.
Anyway, Farouk's daughter, with her wealthy industrialist husband,
moved out here to California. However, she experienced great
problems with servant help. She especially was unhappy with her
children's nurse. So I agreed to help her with the problem. Then I
proceeded to write the Prime Minister of Egypt. I was a bit upset
when I did not get an answer to my request for the Egyptian nurse for
Farouk's daughter. At last I heard; the reason for the delay being that
the Prime Minister had fled the country and was being held prisoner.
Nevertheless, he was unable to grant my request.

One time at a lavish party at Herbert Hischmoeller, I was with the
latest queen, Farouk's wife, who wore a dazzling two hundred and fifty
thousand dollar pin. A bit startled at seeing her for the first time, I
blurted, "I've seen you before." Giving me a quick look and a finger
to the lips, she nodded. Yes, I knew her from France when, away from
Fatso, she often kept company with a young Army officer. Not until
now have I repeated this.

There was a British consul general by the name of Harrow. The

General helped get him knighted so that he became Sir Something Harrow. One evening we were at a party. In fact, I believe that Sir Harrow was the host. Anyway, we were seated at a dinner table. I was on one side, Thelma, Lady Furness— she used her title even in America in the old English tradition— was in the middle, and old Harrow was on the other side. After a while I noticed Lady Furness was sitting on my dress; I quickly called it to her attention and she moved. Again it happened and then when finally it happened again, I got up and went to Harrow. "Now see here," I exclaimed, "it's one thing to keep pinching a woman's bottom at the dinner table, but it is quite another when that woman keeps sitting on my expensive gown and ruining it in an effort to avoid your pinching." He got up in anger and moved to another seat at the table. Many times I saw him later, but instead of his usual friendliness he would murmur only a polite "Good morning, Lady Lawford." As for Lady Furness, I question her breeding. No true lady would allow herself to be pinched more than once!

Her twin sister, Gloria Vanderbilt, and Lady Furness are so different— in looks and brains. It wasn't so long ago that Lady Furness came here for tea. The object of her visit was to buy jade tile from me to tile her bath. Is she *mad?!!* Jade tile for her bath— even the Queen doesn't have *jade* tile for an entire bath!

The Maharajah of Koputulah once went to Madrid, Spain, where he saw on the stage the beautiful dancer named Anita Delgado. She was only about fifteen or sixteen, but he felt he must have her. After their marriage she appeared with him everywhere in the most magnificent clothes. I loved her Paris ballgown which she wore with marvelous emeralds that matched her eyes. Although she lacked background and breeding, she managed to slide into her new role well. However, after about five or six years of marriage to the Rajah, she noticed a change in his attitude toward her fading youth. Finally, she admitted to me that he had tried to poison her. That attempt failed, but she was in great fear of the next attempt. I advised her to slip down to the docks and board a ship bearing a Union Jack.

"Hello y'all, how are y'all doing?" That's what Texas oilman Buddy

Fogelson used to say to me always. Many times I asked him what "y'all" meant. He would laughingly retort, "Y'all means all of you." He was a dear man who was so much fun. Buddy would often asked me, "If you were not married to the General, who would you marry?" While he waited for me to say "you," I would exclaim, "Silly boy!" He once told me that he had voted me the woman he would most like to be with alone on a deserted island. I don't think his wife Greer Garson cared for me.

Mahatma Gandhi— oh, I loathe him! Near the end he would hardly speak a word to me. And once his son came to visit me in my drawing room. I refused to recognize him. I am not an unkind woman, but I must draw the line sometime somewhere. I can remember when Gandhi— pronounced *gundi*— first began to fast. I was interested in his doctrines and his followers. So we investigated a bit on our own in order to draw our conclusions. This famous fast— supposedly the world's longest— was basically a fake. First of all, he was given a piece of sugar cane twice a day for cleaning his teeth. Of course, he ate the sugar cane. Then since water in India is terrible— so easy to get cholera— he was given plenty of fruit juices to drink. This added to his strength. But the most astounding fact of all is his use of opium. He was married to a tiny, illiterate girl who visited him twice each day during fast. Under her very long fingernails she brought him bits of opium. They sometimes used this same opium to endure long battle periods.

Ghandi usually claimed to be an Indian— that is, born in India— but it was well known that he was really from South Africa. He got thrown out of South Africa because he was a troublemaker.

One of the admirals in charge of the Royal Navy there in Bombay had two daughters. Once at a large ball I christened one Polly Plain and Tuppence Colored for the other. The title stuck! Why, I remember one young man came up and asked me for dance number four and five. I looked at him coldly. "You asked me to dance after just dancing with Polly Plain?"

I think Polly Plain went back to England; no, she went to Spain. Anyway, Tuppence, who was left alone in Bombay without her sister, had two girlfriends visiting her. The guests wanted to go out to see and hear Ghandi. It is much like the guru— Yogananda of today with his transcendental meditation. Gandhi was in all the papers; he was like the hippies here, you see, and everyone wanted to see the hippies. So out they went to see him in a village called The Ashram. And Gandhi was nearly always there with nothing but a *dotee* on. A dirty-looking, horrible man, he used a white hat like Nehru has.

Gandhi was a marvelous hypnotist and he took one of the girlfriends aside and completely hypnotized her. She didn't know she was being hypnotized, but she was hypnotized. He said to her, "You will never leave here." The first thing he did was to make her his attendant. If anything was to be done with his slop, she was to go empty those in the morning. And that was his revenge because he didn't like the English. The Commander-in-chief, the Viceroy, the Queen— no one could get her away. Why the Viceroy— what was his name?— Harding— Lord Harding didn't send soldiers and take her back— except that according to law she was twenty-one. She gave up in order to sit at Gandhi's feet. Then after a bit here came Cann, the new Viceroy; but they couldn't do anything about her. So hypnotized, she stayed there until his death.

There was a large party at a downtown hotel— it was to be much fun— a getting together of all sorts of people from every walk of life. That evening I flitted from one person talking to another. Patrick Mahony, the author, made such a to-do over me— you know how I love that kind of flattery. Soon I found myself talking to a small lady dressed in black with a white doily-like collar and an 1837 cameo. Her dark hair was heavily greyed and pulled back in a bun. Her face was totally bare of make-up. She was soft spoken with a trace of an affected accent— what accent I did not recognize. We talked of Hollywood, flowers, animals— everything. When we were leaving, she said, "I've wanted to meet you and I am very pleased to do so. Thank you so much for an interesting conversation." I grasped her hand and warmly invited her to visit me at my home. "Oh, but I won't," she said. "Of course, you may," I said. "I don't visit people," she said. "You see, my name is Polly Adler!"

Chapter Eight
Fiends and Friends

Edith Russell wrote me today. I told you that we met Miss Russell in Majorca when Peter was quite young. She is of a good family and she never married and she seems to have traveled all over the world. I don't recall her ever working; yet she maintained residence at Claridge's for years and years. Both the General and Peter were quite taken with her and she with them. We often saw her in our travels. She is quite a remarkable woman. My God, she must be a hundred years old! She was an old woman— she had grey hair— when we met her in Majorca. Mine was long and dark at that time— not this reddish-gold color that it is now.

Miss Russell tells me in this letter that she is writing her autobiography. Here is what she says:

> My dear friend,
>   I am terribly busy, but will get a few lines off to you. I am doing my autobiography, and it is a full-time job. My early writings for Cassell's Magazine are all in the British Museum— I was never vain enough to keep any copies.

Ha! Listen to that. "Never vain enough"— Poppycock! She goes on:

My father used to say it is better to have been "a has-been" than "a never was"— I also had quantities of servants in my own home, then went and earned my living, made a tremendous success of it, and by the amount of material I have to put in my autobiography, it is a very nostalgic recollection!

If that isn't "tooting one's own horn," I don't know what is.

She says— listen to this:

The Kennedys are not interested in you so don't let anyone kid you into that delusion which puts you in a paranoic "category." Be normal; you are intelligent but have a phobia.

As to the Kennedys, their origin, their fortune— Peter was lucky to get into that family. As an actor he is mediocre— never an Oscar and as a son you may say he is a failure although he may have his side. You possibly insulted him as you do me and others and he blames you for the scandal attached to his birth.

No doubt your approach to Pat and the children was wrong. You should have sent some toys or sweets and a loving card. Then they would have known "May" was not Rose. How could Pat let her children meet a woman who called old man Kennedy a bootlegger and barefoot Irish etc.

Why that old grey-haired fossil! How dare she downgrade Peter's acting career. Look at this list that *The New York Times* compiled of Peter's movies. "Tis every bit of 50 films on there and it doesn't include his new ones that we've seen... *The April Fools, Buona Sera, Mrs. Campbell...* My God! This list doesn't include *Mrs. Miniver,* one of my favorites. Just look at this list:

The White Cliffs of Dover, The Picture of Dorian Gray, Son of Lassie, Cluny Brown, Two Sisters from Boston, It Happened in Brooklyn, My Brother Talks to Horses, Good News, Easter Parade, On an Island With You, Julia Misbehaves, Little Women, The Red Danube, Please Believe Me, Royal Wedding, Just This Once, Kangaroo, You for Me, The Hour of 13,
It should Happen to You, Never so Few, Ocean's Eleven, Exodus, Pepe, Sergeants 3, Advise and Consent, The Longest Day, Dead Ringer, Sylvia, Harlow, The Oscar, A Man Called Adam, Salt and Pepper, Lord Jeff, A Yank at Eton, etc.

I told you, Edith, as a young lady, was aboard the Titanic when it sank— sometimes I wish she had gone under with it. You'd think she was the only person on board. Every year they interview her— the Cunard Line— on BBC. She speaks many languages fluently—

French, German, Italian. And she worked with Arthur J. Rank as an advisor on the "Titanic" motion picture. There was another one about her Titanic experiences— something like "It Happened One Night." She was the girl in the story that had a ceramic pig that had a little key in its stomach that she would wind up and it would play music. She was about to board the lifeboat when she remembered her little clay pig left behind in her stateroom. So she dashes back to get the pig and it played soothing music until she and the others were rescued from the lifeboat. Isn't that a charming story? I think it's true and I think she still has the little pig.

But Edith says in the letter:

> Why should Pat Lawford envy you? What have you that she hasn't got? She has beauty, position, a tremendous fortune, and youth. Why should she envy you— ridiculous!

Ha! Pat Lawford envies my birth— breeding— education— of course, she would like my *pedigree!!!!*

Listen to what that bitch writes me:

> Your "Royal School" omitted courtesy and kindness... no wonder people avoid you. It's rare for a "lady" of breeding to be so uncouth...

> You need a muzzle... Truly you are a sick and sad person needing medical care...

> ... I have been courteous in my replies to you, with the exception of my letters trying to restrain your class prejudice, a thing that went out of style with Queen Victoria— there is no such thing any more, either in England or in America, unfortunately.

> If I get any more insolent letters from you, I will bury you in a nice big tomb, and slam the door.

This is the last straw:

> Let Peter fight his own battle about the illegitimacy stuff, and rest assured that no Kennedy is going to acknowledge that their Sister or

Daughter married a Bastard, and that the children are those of a
Bastard— it is not to their interest, but the more popular Peter gets,
and the more money he makes in his Night Clubs, the more someone
will start any evil rumours— it won't be the Kennedys.

Again, remember, Peter's name is not Lawford on his Passport;
maybe it is now— it wasn't years ago, and he definitely married under
the other name. I have told you that the entire Kennedy family grabbed
me in Florence asking me the details of his other name, and that I had
defended Peter and you at the time; this was in 1960.

I don't have to put up with this. That bitch— she is so free with
her opinions and advice. You know what happened to her once? She
was going to buy a suite of rooms once. She excitedly described them
to the General and me. She told all about the walls and ceilings being
done in red velvet and mirrors. Then she told about some other
strange things— in the suite were whips, manacles, cat-o-nine tails!
Imagine her surprise when upon investigation she almost bought a
brothel. A bordello! That shows her judgment.

As for Peter's illegitimacy, the Kennedys did not start that.
Bartholomew, as you know, started it, and the fact that Peter was
married under a different name than Lawford, which was widely
publicized in the newspapers, suggested that his father was other than
Sir Sydney. You wrote me that Peter's father was a drug-addict,
therefore you had kept his name from Peter, to which I answered you
that Sir Sydney, having accepted support, presents and attention from
Peter over the years showed great cowardice in not going to Nevada and
quietly taking out papers of adoption so that the boy's passport would
have been in order. I don't doubt but what Peter is perfectly legitimate,
but his conception may have been by other than Sir Sydney. However,
he was born while you were Sir Sydney's wife, and some legal form
should have been gone through. All this is none of my business.

I have had enough of her vicious meddling in my business. Let her
think that my arthritis has made me an invalid. After all, arthritis is
supposed to be set off by the emotions and that old bitch has no
business upsetting me with her letters and newspaper articles. Send
her a letter attached to this stuff and say:

Looked over. Letter, papers returned. Anything "needling" or
controversial are not submitted to an invalid by Doctor's Orders.
Incidentally Her Ladyship does not know Mr. Kennedy and never sees
her son or "in-laws."

Temporary Acting Secretary
X

Sign your name and send it to "Miss Russell, Embassy Court Hotel, 31 Queen's Gate 31, London, S.W.7, England.

Old John Farquhar— the professor— what a bore and so tight with his money! But you know his pedigree is almost as long as mine. His father brought his mother and the two boys from England. The old man set himself up in a suite of rooms at the Fairmont in San Francisco and told the wife to go to hell. Later the younger boy attended Harvard Law School making all A's. John himself became a professor at Cal Tech. What an awful drinking problem the younger brother had. So bad that finally John had to lock him in the house. Finally, at the age of twenty-six, the boy committed suicide. Princess Midvani (that bitch!) was so kind to invite John to stay at her house to recover from the tragedy. Did you know that the Princess kept her husband in a little house behind her house? Anyway, John Farquhar snubbed her. Ha!

John discovered a marvelous cancer cure that was tried in Montreal hospitals, and if the cases were treated in time, they were given fifty percent chance of recovery.

However, the American Medical Association would not approve it. I suggested that he send the case to England, but the AMA blocked its export from the United States. Still using my old head, I had John send it first to Canada and from there it was sent to London. John himself flew to England, but with very little success. I asked him, "Why didn't you tell me of your trip? I would have gotten you an introduction to the Queen's doctors of Harley Street."

Living with John was Roger Keys, son of Sir Roger Keys of great naval fame and considerable wealth. Young Keys gave up all— his estate, Eton, honor— to come live with John. It smells of fish to me; doesn't it to you? But I must remain worldly. I can't imagine any woman *or* man wanting to live with John! Anyway, young Keys went to England and gained audience with the Queen because they were rather good friends. You know people in the Royal Circle are like you and me. He told her of me and of John's cancer cure. The Queen agreed to test it in her hospitals. It still allows a fifty-fifty chance on the English people using it in time. When I ask about his money from the cure, John says, "It takes time in testing." If I probe anymore, he spits out, "None of your business!" A fine thank you! You know he owns the property that Sears and Roebuck is built on. I asked him what they paid; he said, "Oh, I don't know." Honestly, how he exasperates and bores me!

Once I met her at Ontra Cafeteria with Mrs. Keaton— Thelma Keaton. With her was a woman in gold lame skin-tight capris— the kind you have to oil your legs to get into. What an outfit with tons of gaudy and jingling bracelets. All the men were giving her "knowing" leers and even a whistle or two. She called herself "Gigi" Jordan or something like that; I called her "Golden Girl." I was very embarrassed. After all, I must think of my station in life— no general's lady is seen in the company of an obvious tart.

Another time I was in the Beverly Hills Ontra— they serve the vegetables that I eat— when I saw Thelma Keaton. Isn't she kin to that movie comedian called "Stonyface?" I proceeded swiftly to my seat. "Lady Lawford! Lady May!" she screamed all across the dining room. After dining with me, Thelma made some excuse about her husband being ill and that she must go to him. So I was left with her woman companion. She looked like that actress that took up with Spencer Tracy. She was evidently Mexican— Mimi Olvera was her name— and she had married into the founding family of Los Angeles, the Olivera of Olivera Street. However, they were divorced. Anyway, we spoke little— she spoke pigeon Spanish, pigeon French, and pigeon English— and when I got up to leave, she followed me to my Thunderbird. She said she had nothing to do for more than two hours so could she sit in my motor car. I said, "Oh, no," and invited her to my drawing room to sit and pass the time. After a while she began looking at my wall of personal friends portraits.

"Isn't that Queen Mother Mary?" she asked.

"Yes, it is," I answered, "I only met her once and found her very charming; however, the General knew her and her husband as well."

Then with a wild look in her eyes, Mimi Olvera said, "Queen Mary, Queen Mary, Queen Mary, you must die! You must die!"

All the time she was grabbing at my throat. She had begun to press quite hard when in the door came Paul Simqu, Peter's public relation man. Seeing my plight, he managed to pull her away from me. My throat had dark marks for quite a while. Imagine my surprise when I discovered that she had been in the mental hospital— Camarillo for three years previously.

Later, Thelma Keaton and I were in Robinson's Department Store and Thelma took me to her— she was working there— saying, "May, you remember Mimi Olvera?" My God, I was ready to run. Such nerve! I had my lawyers, Nessin and Belli, instruct the Keatons to stop harassing me. Mr. Keaton denied the whole thing. Do you know what he did? He saw my picture of DeGaulle whom I knew when he was quite young.

"What are you doing with a picture of that crook?" he asked.

The nerve of calling a friend of mine "a crook" in my own drawing room! Those Keatons just do not know how to appreciate royalty— even minor royalty!

Don't even mention the name of Princess Midvani in front of me. That bitch! Let's drop the subject. Perhaps the only woman friend I have is Mrs. Place. She used to be an opera singer under the name of Marguerite Reise, I think. She told me that she once sang with the New York City Opera Company and the richest man in America proposed to her after seeing her perform on stage. Anyway, Marguerite is not young anymore and her health is failing. Isn't it sad when you are old and alone?

Guess who woke me in the middle of the night? My friend Adrian. He is really the Marquis d'Uzbekke or Aly Adrialysis Khan or something. I can't pronounce it so I call him Adrian. He goes back to Genghis Khan. Anyway, he was telling me of his aunt, Lady Victoria Stevenson out in Claremont. Lady Victoria, who I believe is a cousin to the Queen, has been ill. Why does Adrian insist upon wearing rings on every finger? No wonder people consider him strange in this country. Adrian has taken some of my antiques and paintings saying that he would sell them for me, but I don't know about him. If he is really a friend, I wish he would find more reasonable hours to visit me.

Herbert is one of the few friends that I have left— or even alive. I think his full name is Baron Herbert Kamphuyzen van Hischemoeller or something like that. His pedigree is quite legitimate as is his title; Herbert's mother is one of the grand dames of the Netherlands. I used to think that Herbert only invited the General and me to this parties because of the "handle"— you know, "sir" and "lady." However, after twenty years of friendship he must truly enjoy the company. Speaking of company, did you know that Herbert's spice company produces all the spices in the world— well, almost all. That's how he got the title of "Spice King." Now I hear that he owns so much of the Ivory Coast that they are going to make him Consul General.

Poor Herbert. I've heard this terrible story that I don't know if it is true. When he was younger, the story goes that he was married to a beautiful show-girl type— like Brenda Joyce or Joyce Brenda— whatever. One night while lying next to him in bed as he was sleeping, she put a gun to her head and blew her brains out. Can you imagine waking up to that! Like I say, I don't know if it is true, but if it did happen, oh, poor Herbert.

Herbert has a lovely home up on Summit Ridge, just above Pickfair. He has some marvelous furnishings and beautiful tapestries. But something is strange: downstairs are little cubicles, one next to the other, which contain a bed and a bath where Herbert lets young men live. It smells of fish to me. Living with Herbert is a very handsome young man named Mark Nixon. I danced with Mark at one of their Christmas parties and he is a divine dancer.

If you want something done and done correctly, just call on Herbert. He's been wonderful to me since I've been alone. When I wanted my money back from the George Putnam Fund, Herbert got my investment back quickly. And when that car salesman Mr. Franks took all my valuables, it was Herbert who demanded and got them back for me. Truly Herbert is a dependable friend.

Thank goodness for Patrick Mahony, probably the only old friend that I have left; I mean a real friend of long standing. Patrick's background equals mine. He is Irish, but was born in London. His half brother is Sir Arthur Bliss, Keeper of the Queen's Music, and his sister was Lady Cunard, married to the shipping magnate. Patrick's early years were spent in association with famous writers, Maurice Maeterlinck and Lord Dunsany.

Such a beautiful garden Patrick's mother, Mrs. Frances Bliss had at her small estate on Pepper Tree Lane in Santa Barbara. And always she had some lovely and interesting guests— royalty, writers, poets, dramatists, musicians, and artists. I adored visiting there. And it is little wonder that Patrick should be so good as an author, playright, and humorist.

Although many people remember Patrick's book, *Breath of Scandal,* best, I just love his *It's Better in America.* He delivers an amusing lecture on the merits of life in America. You remember I said that I never wanted to go back to England to live. The plumbing never works and the food is atrocious. It's all very beastly.

Patrick also writes about extrasensory perception and related psychic phenomena. In fact, he was decorated by the President of Ireland for his writing concerning E.S.P. Ever since I lived in India, I have been interested in reincarnation, karma, automatic writing, and things of the psychic world. Patrick writes beautifully about these subjects.

Always Patrick's parties are a delight. He seems to know everyone who is interesting. And such flattery— he always flatters me. "Cut out your blarney," I say to him, but secretly I love it.

Chapter Nine

Lady Lawford
The Writer, The Actress

There was a marvelous picture called "the Bengal Lancers," about our famous British group. I believe General Jay was the advisor. But, oh, what a terrible thing happened in the end— at the burial of the hero, they pinned the Victoria Cross on the hero's horse. The Victoria Cross is the highest honor given by English much like the Purple Heart or Bronze Star that you Yanks give. But to a *horse!* The General and I just roared at the thought of it— both with laughter and anger. Anyway, a new picture was now being filmed— a very important film at the time called "Hong Kong."

One morning I told the General that I was going to visit the set; he simply said, "Suit yourself." Once there, I went up to the star Ronald Reagan and offered my services as Army advisor since my entire family is of the Army. Of course, I asked for no remuneration. Reagan was quite surprised to find me the mother of Peter Lawford.

After talking with him for quite a while, he said that it was decided: I should play a leading role in the picture. "Oh no," said I, "I only came to make certain that you did not pin the Victoria Cross on a horse." Nevertheless, in addition to my advising in Army matters I also played a part in the film. I remember one scene in which I, a bereaved widow, scream as they bring my dead husband by. "They've killed him; they've killed my husband!" And then I looked at Reagan and added, "And they've done a damned good job of it!" He broke up. And that was the advent of Mary Sommerville: Actress.

One evening I went to a party alone. The General, knowing it was mainly movie people, did not wish to go. He was also suffering from a bit of influenza. Yet he insisted I not stay with him, but attend "because they are Peter's friends."

While there, some little Jew, an agent, tried to play up to me. He said that he had someone who wished to be introduced to me. I forget the director or producer's name, but I immediately said, "What do you want?" A bit shaken by my abruptness, he stumblingly asked my name. "'Mary Sommerville is my working name, but I'm Lady May Lawford in private life." I told him that I was with Reagan in *Hong Kong* and in *Mr. Peabody and the Mermaid* I was with— oh, what's his name— William Powell.

Anyway, this man complimented my elocution and my diction saying the English pronounce certain words so much better. He especially liked my pronunciation of "Worcestershire sauce." He asked me to come to Metro-Goldwin-Mayer studio at eight-thirty the next morning for make-up and wardrobe for some tests.

During my test, he handed me a script— such a cute script! He raved and raved over my reading and over my posture and regal carriage.

"Do you object to commercials?" he asked, explaining the good money in them.

"No," I said, "but let's cut out the flattery and get down to brass tacks. How much?"

"A hundred dollars a day for an indefinite period of use."

"Well," said I, "that'll buy the cats some liver!" All was settled.

Then, the door opened— Mrs. Patricia Lawford entered. Everyone said "good morning" to her including the man testing me. He then continued to tell her how good I was. She was a bit aghast when she recognized me. Later she and the man went into another room. When the man returned, he was of a totally different attitude. He whispered to me, "The studio limousine will await you out front to drive you home. I'm terribly sorry that things cannot be arranged." That was all the explanation.

From my first acting job— a bit part in *Mr. Peabody and the Mermaid*— I made the grand total of $386.00. The money was not important; I was doing something I loved to do. In fact, I took the money and sent food packages to the needy in England.

I would like to do some more acting. I did a Climax show on television— it was a bit part which allowed me to carry my cat Amber. I got one hundred dollars for that and felt like a million. Peter was just across the hall from the studio where I was acting, but he did not know that I was doing the part. He heard the news later from newspaper reporters.

The General, Peter, and Patricia would be surprised if they knew of the little jobs that I took under another name.

Once I was on Peter's *Thin Man* show. It was a ball really, being on television. But after Peter joined the "Royal Family", they didn't want me to act.

Years ago The Clan let it be known that I'm not popular. While I am strong and healthy, I could and would take a job to make my life a little easier, but for some unknown reason, writing, T.V., pictures, and serving in a store all got put to a stop. Why, I couldn't even sell jewelry for Mr. Tibor. It is really none of Peter's business. He should be used to me by this time. Sometimes I think Peter should have had Whistler's mother. Anyway, there was not anymore acting for me. The Clan— or Rat Pack— appears to have fixed it so that no agent offers me anything. Why, you remember when I was told I'd be perfect in the Billie Burke part in a remake of *Dinner at Eight.*

But they'll never drive me out. Never!

How does this letter sound to you?

> Dear Sir:
> The reason I bothered you is I am trying to make a "come back" with my writing.

Some years ago I wrote for the following papers: *Daily Mail, Daily Express, Daily Mirror, The Star Evening News, Liverpool Post, Weekly Telegraph, The Queen, Woman Magazine, Brittania, British Empire Review, Times of India, Swiss Tattler, American Weekly, Prediction,* etc.

In London, I had two agents (both deceased now); I also had a typist secretary. Now I am alone.

I am the widow of General Lawford and mother of actor Peter Lawford, who was the brother-in-law of the president, J. F. Kennedy.

Sincerely,

Lady May Lawford

This is one of my earlier writings. It isn't so bad, is it?

At a London hairdresser's the other day to have my small son's hair cut, I was struck by the fact that the modern child lacks nothing in the matter of comfort; and I could not contrast the treatment of their well-groomed heads to the tortures we endured in my dim and distant nursery days! Here they sat on their painted, prancing wooden horses, covered by a cloak, a medley of pictures of trains, animals, and aeroplanes; with a picture-book in their hands; while their hair was expertly attended to.

One fairy-like thing of 6 was having her "perm" set, "just like Mummy," in a net with a dryer. Another tot of 4 bent his neck to the clipper "just like Dad." They went through the series of shampoo, cut, etc., just as grave as could be, their eyes occasionally wandering to "nannie" or "mummie" seated nearby. All was peace and decorum until Posey arrived. Posey was about 3; she wore yellow crepe-de-chine and a bonnet trimmed with white rosebuds; and she said, loud and long, that today at any rate, she would not submit to a cut, wave, or any old thing— and said it in a loud voice to all-and-sundry within the radius of two floors! Her mother said, "Pops, dear!" Her nurse said, "Miss Posey!"; the lady-barber said, "No, darling!" But Posey was well away and indulged in a real go of hysterics and chucked herself about with real abandon! I would love to know if Posey won the day. But alas, I had to leave— her shrieks followed me for the length of two departments!

I suppose that I was ahead of time or perhaps old-fashioned as this writing reveals:

Time was when little girls had ringlets, hair ribbons, spotted muslin, pinafores and patent shoes, all designed to train them in self-respect, tidiness, and beauty. Now a crew cut, T-shirt, denim slacks and sandals is standard equipment— in spite of the 22nd chapter of Deuteronomy!

Children were supposed to learn scripture at their "mother's knee," but if those knees are under an office desk for eight long hours— then no family prayers; no grace before meals! So, knowing no better, the child joins the ranks of The-Take-All-And-Give-Nothing-Christian, and if some "nosey" old grandparent suggests on Sunday that they should attend church or Sunday school, they get: What? ME take them? I work all week!... I need my rest!... Baloney! Go make the coffee— and hand me the funnies.

With this bloodless revolt of women, the men have retreated and their slogan is: "The line of least resistance!" Can you wonder when they are bludgeoned into submission by the Club of Alimony, wielded by some "blond bird-brain" who, the first time she is refused a request, shrieks: "Divorce!" "Mental cruelty!" and all the trimmings.

Man, of course, is not guiltless, but quarrels would not last long if the wrong was all one-sided. Heaven alone knows when, where, and how this will all end. We can only hope that some intelligence might arise in the women of today, to direct their return to the lovely, gentle, God-fearing people we know and admired in our childhood days.

The General loved to gamble. He once asked me not to bother him because he had twelve thousand dollars on the board. He particularly enjoyed roulette. But he was quite lucky. Many of my bracelets and my three thousand dollar diamond watch he won at the table. Frequently in Monte Carlo he would be busy working "his system" so he could not dance with me. At these times he would give the Russian princes— who were in exile— thirty or forty dollars to dance with me for the evening. Those Russians are wonderful dancers, but terrible bores.

I was society editor for Monte Carlo so that led to this later article:

Things, more unbelievable than incidents in Hollywood, happen in Monte Carlo. A typist, lured no doubt by romantic dreams, fired by much of the cloying literature on the subject, came down on her yearly holiday to "try her luck." Down to last 100 francs, she was found at midnight weeping on the terrace, by a baron from somewhere in the Balkans, who dried her tears, married her— and a week later died from an overdose of Veronal, leaving her all his money— which Madame la Baronne is fast doing her best to give to the casino!

A princeling of a poverty-stricken Royal House, on a visit to Paris, married the pretty daughter of the woman who manicured his nails so delightfully— and returned with her to Monte Carlo, where she is fawned on by the new-comers and cold-shouldered by those in the know.

Any small Royal can live for nothing at Monte Carlo. There are some who lunch and dine free, and have their names in the society papers as

having done so seven days a week. They have no expenses other than
rent and busfares, and most of the people, who curtsey to them at a gala
dinner, remember to forget having sat next to them on the bus ride to
Nice!

The number of countesses from Chicago is overwhelming. Newly
outnumbered by the Papal Princesses from Pennsylvania. If a newcomer
enquires where the male portions of the titles are, you hear: "Sadie's
husband? Oh, he went out on his ear the week after the wedding. She
didn't need him! She has her grandad's canning business."

Oh, isn't that a beastly picture of me on that article about Monte
Carlo? I look like an old dowager— but my jewels and furs were good.
It is an interesting article, don't you think?

My experience as Peter's required parent on the set led me to write
this article. I call it "The Joys and Sorrows of a Film Parent!"

There's a law which is designed to protect movie moppets from
overwork, etc. which says that a parent or guardian must be on the set
with them. I, being guardian, accompanied him to the studios and I
never imagined I would be so entertained and amused as I was watching
the various mothers primp and brush-up their off-spring. It is a thing
that ordinary movie-goers miss.

The mothers at the movies, who cast envious eyes on the screen's
glamour children, have no idea of the wear and tear of nerves expended
by their parents; of the struggle to keep them in the glare of the "Kleig
lights." Long before that "eldorado" known as a contract is reached,
there are countless hours in photographers' studios, conferences with
hairdressers on perms and peroxide, dressmakers to be persuaded and
cajoled, etc. And yet more and more weary hours in agents' offices,
countless battles to get past secretaries, long bus rides with a tired,
whimpering child and a string of tomorrows to look forward to. The
week-ends all too short for rest and repose. Then the breathless moment
when the casting director's eye is at last on little Gwendolyne of the
"marmalade locks," and mama, about to swallow her heart, feels: She's
got it!... she hasn't!... she has! And then Gwendolyne, bloated with
candy, weary from "frock-tugging," and hair-combing looks the director
coldly in the eye and says: "Nuts to you..." she hasn't. Then spanking
for one and tears for two, and off we go again.

The next thrill: When a producer and director confer as to the looks
and merits of the juvenile aspirant, and he looks her over, much like a
prize pig in a fair! Mama mentally hashes Gwendolyne's chances.

Conscious of aching feet, her home containing unmade beds and
unwashed dishes, plus a querulous, most unsympathetic attitude to this
fool movie business by a practical husband, she tries to insist that the
director has long been looking for just Gwendolyne and that his idea

that she should be four feet high instead of three, and have red hair
instead of blond is just a whim he'd better forget. She's read the script,
she knew it fitted Gwendolyne the minute she saw it and so on.
Result:... she hasn't. Next time, the agent immune to mothers and their
methods with their young, leave mama at home, reading the film
magazine. Result: This time she has. Signed, sealed and engaged for the
duration of a picture Gweny is delivered to the set where, amidst more
"frock-tugging, hair-fussing," unbelievable noise, Gweny is supposed to
give her calm and undivided attention to her lessons and the film and
school room. Sick with excitement, nervous to the verge of tears which
finally come to relieve the tension, Gweny smudges her make-up into
her dress, and her eyes, and hair, thereby earning the active hate of
make-up and wardrobe, to say nothing of the lady in charge of her
education. Mother goes to bat for her offspring demanding rest and
orange juice. Entirely ignoring the shout of "Juice, please!" she
eventually manages to get in the hair of everyone from the director
downwards.

A few days later, when Mother has found a kindred soul to compare
operations with, and Gweny has discovered a boy to trade candy for
cake, all is serene and Gweny is off to a good start and she finished the
picture where she appears on the screen for a quarter of a second to the
indignation of her adoring parents. Then here we go again. As it was in
the beginning, Gweny is dragged from interview to interview— at the
end of the year when Oscars are given out, the parents of these children
deserve a special one— and how!

Ever since I have lived in India, I have been interested in the
occult, ESP, psychic phenomena, and the like. Anyway, Margaret
Fuller is the very nice woman who is editor of *Fate* Magazine, a
group of true stories about the unknown. Mrs. Fuller, who seems so
nice from her letters, published some of my articles in her wonderful
magazine— I never miss an issue. And best of all she always uses with
my stories a good picture of me. Look at that. Isn't that good of me? I
think that it is my very favorite picture of me.

This story is called "Whose Hand Holds Mine?"

I fell asleep, alone in a locked room, and awoke in the dawn to the
distinct feelings that someone was holding my hand.

The day before I had moved into a new house and had chosen the
largest, and what I judged to be the coolest bedroom as the normal
temperature for a mid-summer night on the northwest frontier of India
is around 116 degrees.

It was a stifling hot night. There was not a breath of air; only now
and again I heard the drone of a mosquito. I took a shower, poured

myself some ice water and eventually fell asleep.

I awoke slowly and naturally; my arms were flung above my head. I was aware that a cool, strong hand was clasping mine. My husband? Had he returned unexpectedly? No... in the early morning light I looked at my right hand and I could see no other hand. Still I felt a distinctly cool, firm grip.

Sitting up in bed I rubbed my hand, telling myself that it must be some trick of circulation. Then slowly, as if loath to let go, the feeling of the handclasp faded away.

Wide awake now and more than a little uneasy, I sprang out of bed. Although it was only 5:00 o'clock, I ordered coffee and my horse. At the time I gave orders for my bed and belongings to be moved into another room.

As I rode through the woods in that cool dawn I pondered over the happenings of the night; certainly it had not been a dream. After breakfast I wrote my experience to my husband, General Sir Sydney Lawford, who was away inspecting troops in another part of India. I was tempted to join him but felt it stupid to run away from an intangible sensation.

That same afternoon, while walking the dogs, I met a very old woman. She was bent almost double as she moved about gathering wood and berries which were probably to be her evening meal. After talking with her for a few moments, I held out some silver and asked her if she knew any stories about the village. "That house," I said, indicating the one I had just rented, "what was in it before white sahibs came here?"

"That is a sad house," she answered. "There is no evil in it, only a 'happy sadness.'"

"Tell me more," I requested, giving her some more small change.

After tying the money in her sash, she told me this story:

Years before the present house was built, the residence of a very nice Indian merchant had stood in the same place. This merchant had an only and lovely daughter who fell in love with a penniless young man who was good and kind. However, the merchant would have none of this youth, and arranged to marry his lovely child to a man almost as old as himself— a wealthy man who already had two other wives. The girl cried and protested in vain. And when it became clear that there was no alternative since the girl's wedding was to take place the next day, the two young lovers took poison. Their bodies were found on the morning of the scheduled wedding— dead on the floor of her room, hand in hand.

This experience of mine occurred many years ago in India, when nothing of the sort had ever happened to me before. The memory of the incident would be fresh in my memory even if it were not kept so by the fact that sometimes I still wake up with the feeling of a cool, strong hand gripping mine.

Here is another story called "House with the Earthbound Spirits":

My son, Peter, was about eight-years-old when our little family returned from a voyage to Tahiti, Australia, and the Hawaiian Islands.

Arriving in London, we were met by the usual downpour and leaden skies; it was anything but warm, although it was August.

Among my mail, I received a letter from a friend who wished to rent us his house on the island of Madeira for the coming winter. Even though we were half-unpacked, we all decided to take the house. My husband, General Sir Sydney Lawford, booked our passages on the next outgoing steamer.

We were enchanted with the house. The garden and grounds were full of Lilies-of-the-Nile, plus Bougainvillaea in all shades of glorious color. In addition, the butler, cook and two upstairs maids went with the home.

We settled happily into our new environment, prepared to enjoy tennis, drives, bathing and other recreation available on the delightful island. The house was too large for us— four or five bedrooms and bathrooms, a drawing room which the servants called The Ballroom. My husband and I slept in a large room with three windows overlooking the sea; it also had three doors with glass transoms opening onto the corridor. Peter slept in a smaller room just off ours, with no doors and separated only by an archway with curtains.

After we had lived there two or three months, we were invited to a big Portuguese wedding and did not return to the house until about one o'clock. As our son was already asleep, we went quickly to bed.

At four o'clock, I awoke with a start. Peter stood by the side of my bed and his white, China-silk pajamas sticking to his body as if he had gone swimming in them.

"What on earth?" I gasped.

"I can't sleep in my room. Someone keeps looking at me. Let me stay here— please!" Peter pleaded.

After rubbing him dry and changing his pajamas, I put him to sleep on one of the couches in our bedroom. When General Lawford woke in the morning and saw him there, he said, "A fine way to spoil the child!" and indicated he did not believe Peter's story.

Every night, our son went to bed in his room and every morning we found him covered by one of his blankets on the couch in our room. After a week or ten days of this, I, too, began to wake up with the feeling that someone was watching me. My chiffon nightgown would be clinging to my body and my pillow wet with perspiration.

I awakened my husband who murmured, "Mass hysteria," and went back to sleep.

However, about a week later, around midnight, he woke me and said someone or something was looking at him from the transoms.

Next day, my husband told the butler to glue some brown paper on the side of the three transoms and that night he removed the keys after locking the bedroom doors.

The following morning, I awoke, grateful for an undisturbed night, only to look at the floor and find it covered with pieces of brown paper— paper torn from the inside of the transom by unseen hands.

After some discussion, my husband and I decided to take the next ship to London. The friends we had made on the island then gave us a nice farewell party.

At the farewell party, an elderly gentleman said to me, "I wondered how long you would stay there. Six months is about the limit!"

When I asked him why, he promptly answered, "That house is full of earthbound spirits— two murders and a suicide in the big bedroom!"

And "I Couldn't Close The Door" is another true story of mine published in *Fate*.

During the reign of King Edward VII (the exact date escapes me), I made many friends at the finishing school I attended— The Princess Helena College at Ealing, near London.

My best and dearest schoolfriend was the daughter of a clergyman in a small town in the heart of the English country. At school, during our "morning break for milk or juices," she would tell us tales of her home in the vicarages; how, after dark, walking down the long stony passages, always dimly lit, "someone" or "something" would push her gently to one side; how a door would open but there would be no one in the room, just a sound of someone breathing as if they had run up a hill fast. She told us she never could have a pet cat or dog. They would stay for a bit, then run away, yelping— the hair on their backs standing up in terror.

One incident made us laugh. Very early one morning, before dawn, the Vicar, hearing a noise, went to investigate and fell over a carpetbag which was full of burglar's tools and implements. The burglar obviously had left in a hurry. The thing that walked the corridor must have pushed him also, so that he fled like the household pets.

Many years later, while back in England on a leave from India, I ran into my friend at the home of a mutual friend in London. She said her father had retired and had bought the old Vicarage where he and she continued to live, and that the people of the country town had built a fine new house for the new Vicar.

In due course, I went to stay with my friend for a long weekend; my husband remained in London. The day of my arrival was one of "those days" that most of us experience. It rained! (In England, it always does!) I lost my hat box, smashed my watch, and arrived in a disgruntled mood.

After a session in the library with the old Vicar and some fine dry sherry, I was escorted upstairs to dress for dinner. While brushing out my long hair, I glanced at the door. It was open. So I shut it in case one of the maids should pass by. A minute later, about to give a final look at myself in the long mirror, I saw that the door was wide open again!

"These old-fashioned locks!" I muttered as I slammed the door and promptly forgot it.

I got to bed around midnight, after an endless chat— going back over the years. I had acquired the habit in the Orient and I kept a dim night light in my room. In the early morning hours, I suddenly woke up to find the door wide open! I told myself I was certain I had shut it, but to make sure this time, I removed the key after locking the door. I placed the key on my bedside table. Then I slept soundly until I woke to find a trim maid at my bedside with my early morning tea.

"How," I asked, glancing at the door key on my bedside table, "did you get in?"

"The door was wide open," she replied.

After breakfast, we went to the village and while my friend was in a shop, I fled into the post office and sent a telegram to my husband asking to be recalled by telephone *at once!!*

Sorry as I was to leave my dear friend and the comfortable old-world atmosphere of the charming vicarage, I just couldn't take the proximity of "the thing," or "It" that so obviously owned the house and to whom locked doors meant nothing.

Chapter Ten

Whatever Happened To Lady Lawford?

The whole of the thing began when Jack Kennedy began his campaign for President. You see, Peter and the Clan (Frank Sinatra, Dean Martin, Sammy Davis, etc.) tried to get me out of the country during the campaign by offering me an expense-paid trip— one way— to visit my sister Gretta in Africa. They're very age-conscious, those Kennedys. They didn't want me around because I didn't look like Whistler's Mother.

During that time— the election campaign— I even had to tell columnist Mike Connolly, "I can't talk any more because they might deport me." When he asked who *they* were, I simply asked him, referring to my relative— by marriage— Jack Kennedy, "Your President couldn't change the law just on account of me, could he?"

This hidden hand! I have many good friends who are afraid of the Syndicated and hidden hand. One friend who investigated said, "The Kennedys want you out of their hair."

When I came here, all the neighbors came "dripping honey"—

"When can we see Peter and the kids, Mrs. Lawford?" After two years, they began to look at me and smile in a sad way, as no one came to see me. Certainly my name was Lawford, but I was "bats," "off my rocker," "lost my mind," and so on, and the ideas of being connected with J.F.K. was in my head! No wonder Peter took my car away— and they were about to sign a paper asking to put me away in Camarillo— or use his influence with J.F.K to do so. The landlady of the "don't-want-to-get-involved" type throws me out.

Little peasants, they think that because I am different in my speech, my clothes, and my background, that I think that I am better than they are. However, I am always gracious to them if they speak to me. Really, you can't blame the uninformed neighbors for going along with the taboo.

Still, I have had some unpleasant phone calls such as "You old phoney— you are not Lady Lawford" and "Even your family won't accept you."

The neighbors must think I either drink, use drugs or keep some man. Since Pat and Peter came to live here, I have lost many friends. However, as God is my witness, I have done no evil to them and do not deserve such inhuman treatment.

For some time past, I have been subjected to a great deal of unpleasantness. I only relate the incidents that can be verified by friends, police or the Federal Bureau of Investigation in case someone suggests "imagination." The following episodes will explain in some measure what I mean.

One day, a man called— I have his name and number— and asked if I could meet him for a business interview in the lobby of the Beverly Hills Hotel. I did. The result of the meeting was this deal: "I offer you a house, three servants, a car, one thousand dollars a month and ten percent of my book publishing business— if you will go and live in Cannes, France."

I stalled and asked a friend to investigate. He found, he said, that "the Kennedy s want you out of their hair." This same friend said Peter, MGM and the William Morris Agency did not want me to publish my book. The friend had been asked to tell me this, seeming the others lack guts or "conscience makes cowards of the bravest!"

I told you about how Peter had those men break into my house to steal the book that I had been writing about Peter and the pictures I had of him. Peter used to fancy himself a girl and delighted in wearing female attire. I had many pictures of this.

I used to ask him, "Are you a homo or something?" At the time of the break-in, he was living with a homo whom he "loaned" a great deal of money, and also put him in a picture in Rome— even chartered his plane. I had nothing to say— I suppose a man must try everything that suits him. If he wants to be a homo, that is his business.

One night— about 11:30— I spoke on the phone to Dean Severance, the actor pal of Peter— in reply to his call. We talked awhile and said good night. I put the phone in its cradle and went to sleep. After midnight, I heard police cars drive up and a voice said, "She's dead." A moment later, a man put a ladder against my window, crashed in the screen and put his head in and said, "You're *not* dead?" Having been raised in a strictly military family, I said some things to him I'd prefer to forget. I got up and let the following procession into the living room: two policemen, several pulmotor attendants, and several ambulancemen. I called for their identifications and asked, "Who sent you?" The reply was "Dean Severance," who then walked in and said, "I heard you have a heart attack at about eleven thirty and throw the phone down, so I knew you were dead and I brought these men." Once everyone had left, I discovered that both the book that I had been writing and the pictures of Peter were missing.

A friend, Mrs. Lee Epstein, who worked in a jewelry shop and knowing I had so little money and would be wanting to buy my grandchildren and Peter and sister Gretta something nice for Christmas, wanted me to get a job and make some Christmas spending money. The man, her boss, Mr. Tibor, seemed delighted to have me with him. I went to work on Monday with an expense account and ten percent commission on sales. All hell broke loose! Cameras! Reporters day and night, calls from London— even reporters on my doorsteps placed pictures and stories in one hundred and twenty-eight papers in the United States and all the London dailies. Friday, Mr. Tibor had obviously been "got at" and said I must leave now for the South of France. He gave no reason for this statement.

Previously, Mr. Tibor gave a cocktail party in my name and a gate-crasher broke in and I saw from his attitude that he was about to put over a "rough house" so I, as hostess, asked him to leave, telling him that he was not invited. When he replied in a rude and belligerent manner, I— accidentally— spilled a couple of drinks on his leg and he left. He was obviously some hoodlum hired to make trouble— but by whom?

How would you enjoy it if people kept saying that you were insane? Look, I even got my doctor to check me and to state his opinion:

> January 17, 1967
> To Whom It May Concern:
> Re: Lady May Lawford
> Lady May Lawford has been under my care for minor medical problems. She has no serious organic disease and is mentally alert.
> Very truly yours,
>
> Harley J. Gunderson, M.D.

On the advice of friends, I went on the Paul Coates television show to prove I was not insane. That very same night, I was kept awake by prowlers, my hose was cut in two pieces, my flowers killed, mud was thrown on the house and my pet cat was stolen.

On the first of December, I developed a chest cold which I neglected until the fifth of December, when I visited Dr. Bethea, my doctor since 1954. He gave me codeine because I coughed all day and night. Next day, since I showed no improvement, he said, "Double the dose." Some days after, I became so dizzy I could hardly walk. Next day, I fell down the stairs and I felt that I had broken ribs, and the doctor, of course, "only accepted emergencies for home calls." I had to shop for groceries and I drove so badly all over the road! After lunch, I put a cushion on the floor and I lay next to the coral-colored couch, too dizzy to stand. A friend, Mrs. Doggett, arrived and, seeing me lying there, evidently called the doctor. He immediately rushed to see me.

When he arrived, Mrs. Doggett said that I was drugged and offered, to fetch my cough mixture. He replied, "Nonsense! Don't you touch anything— she has had a stroke." The doctor then said to us, "Shut up and get out." The house keys were left with neighbors in case of fire or in case of liberation for the cats. He put me in the ambulance that he brought with him.

Drugged and having slept soundly I woke up naked in bed in St. John's Hospital with six or seven nurses. The doctor there said, "Well, you've got your X-rays and you stay there till I tell you to leave in a day or so." I pleaded for my wool dress and glasses and such, which they did. After all left the room, I got up and went into the hall. Three large elevators— all automatic— were in the hall. In one, there were three men in white uniforms; the second elevator was shut; the third was shutting. I just did get in and went down, wearing no shoes or underclothes. The elevator opened and I saw my son and his bodyguard quarreling. Neither would speak to me, so I walked in an opposite direction slowly, as if I were a visitor. As I got to the hall door, I prayed hard. A door opened and a very drunk taxi driver came in. I said, "Hurry up, this is my taxi," and I jumped in. The doctor shouted at me. But, fortunately, we were gone. When I got home, I locked myself in.

The next day, a friend took me to Mr. Melvin Belli's office. Belli said, "That act you put on probably saved your life." He gave me instructions on what to do not to be caught again. Mr. Belli's last instructions were, "Keep one jump ahead and you'll live, but you'll not live long if you do not obey our joint letter!"

Here's the letter with the instructions:

August 12, 1964
Lady Mae Lawford 413 Veteran Avenue Los Angeles CA 90024

Dear Lady Lawford:
   In view of the number of strange and inexplicable things which have happened to you within the last year or so, and because of the possibility of some physical danger to you, it is our suggestion that you conduct your daily activities more or less on the following basis:
   1. That you remain in your home during the night hours, such as,

for example, 6:00 or 7:00 P.M., to approximately 8 A.M. of the following day.

2. That you limit or restrict your visits to hospitals, either as a visitor or as a patient. In the event that you should require emergency medical attention, you could obviously use either an *emergency hospital* or notify the Police Department of your needs.

3. That you remain out of strange neighborhoods.

4. That you select your places to eat with some degree of care, although we understand that you are now having your main meal of the day at Ontra Cafeteria, where you are able to select your own choice of foods. This would seem to be all right.

5. That you refrain as much as possible from any *trips* by *plane, train* or *boat.*

6. That you hold little or no conversation with strangers, or people that you do not know well.

7. That you be very careful about eating or drinking at any afternoon parties, which you may attend.

Basically, we believe that the above are nothing more than common sense safety rules which could be helpful in preventing any unusual incidents such as those which you have advised us have happened to you heretofore. We trust that these suggestions will be helpful to you.

With kindest personal regards, we remain,

Very truly yours,

Confirmed by Melvin Belli, by phone.

On St. Patrick's night, at around nine o'clock, I was reading in my cottage— a Presbyterian church cottage at Wilshire Boulevard on Ashton. The door was ajar for air and suddenly my cat Amber ran out. I quite forgot my orders from Mr. Belli and Mr. Nessen, my attorneys, and I flew out after the cat. As I got to the last step, two men came from the side of the building, grabbed me and pushed me into a car— their hands over my mouth. I sat on the floor and every time we stopped at a red light, they put their hands over my mouth.

We got to a building, went down some steps into a room full of male and female nurses and patients being sick. They stripped my clothes off and gave me a short muslin shift, threw a half-glass of whiskey over me and put me in a kind of cage that fastened from the top. I had many hypos in my arms; later my doctor counted several holes.

I had some medicine that made me dizzy, as if I was in a dense fog. By sheer will power, I did not become unconscious. After sitting in the cage for a long time, a tall man wearing glasses came and peered in at me. He said, "You poor little soul, you don't look drunk." And

when I said, "I am Peter Lawford's mother and I want to go home!"
He said, "God Almighty! What a ghastly error; stay there till I get a
cab, and the man who brought you and I'll see you get home."

Soon after, he gave me a man's shirt— now Princess Midvani has it
along with the shift— and when I got back from changing, I found
the Princess' doctor, Dr. Takamine and a nurse. The medicine in my
body began to take effect and from then on, all is dim and foggy
except that I felt as if I had been run over by a steam roller and I was
covered in big black bruises. Next day, Dr. Takamine called saying
that he would like to see me. So with great pains and difficulty, I went
and he counted the bruises and said, "Another beating and you won't
come out so easily, if at all!"

My own doctor, Dr. Tolle, went to where he thought I had been
taken and found the police who said in a whisper, "The Kennedys,
not a word," and refused comment.

When my cottage was searched by Princess Midvani and two
doctors, no drink of any kind was found. The morning following my
episode, I got all my clothes brought back in a paper bag and left on
the step of my cottage.

Some party planted Communist papers in my home— I mean
really Red. On Paul Simqu's— he was then a public relations man at
UCLA— advice, a friend, Charles Waldo, and I sealed them and
returned them to Mrs. Keaton. Those papers found in the possession
of a British subject would cause me to be deported.

Four very large— at least six feet tall— men tried to enter my house
on Halloween. You Yanks call them "tricksters or treats." Anyway,
they beat on my door, but I wouldn't let them in. So the hoodlums set
off firecrackers, set fire to the trash cans outside and smeared paint on
the windows of my car. I called the police but they ran away before
the officers arrived.

What it is like to be subjected to such indignities— such
annoyances! Oh, the many obscene and horrible phone calls made
most nights at four to five A.M. The phone company has changed my
number once or twice, but it still goes on.

Small things begin to annoy— like the obscene phone calls. Why do people occasionally plaster my front door with dozens of eggs? Thanks goodness, the landlord hosed them away for me.

Since the kidnapping episode by Peter... I have been talked to by the British, French and American press, who are anxious to have the story, and if I get no satisfaction, I will give them the whole horrible mess.

Old people are frequently put in a "nut house" when they are unproductive and cost money. Several people have told me of the ever-increasing fact of persons being railroaded into asylums!

It has been years since Peter has come to see me or called me. He is surrounded in his office by people who hate me. Neither my son nor the office managers will speak, write or reply to my telegrams. I suppose the less I have to do with Peter, his family and his office, the more tranquil I am.

Perhaps I could move to Monte Carlo. Would you come with me? Yes, Monte Carlo would be wonderful. You see, I have already tried to get a "Grace and Favour" apartment in London. Here is my letter and my reply:

January 16, 1967

W.C. Whitlock, M.P. Esquire Controller to H.M. the Queen, Buckingham Palace London, S.W. 1 England

Dear Sir

Please tell me if my background makes me eligible to apply for residence at the "Grace and Favour" Apartments in the British Royal Palaces.

My late husband was General Sir Sidney Barlow Turing Lawford, Royal Fusiliers. His career can be checked at the War Office from Sandhurst to World War I, plus medals and orders, etc.

My late father, Colonel Frederick Brice Bunny, Royal Berkshire Regiment, invalided out after the Boer War (Sandhurst first).

My grandfather Royal Horse Artillery was forty-one years in India during the mutiny, etc. and with his close friend Lord Roberts, he began at Sandhurst also.

My uncle Colonel Frederick Brice Bunny, also Royal Horse Artillery and later in sole charge of Coast Defenses, G.B., can be checked at War Office. He died in London.

My only brother, Lt. Brice Bunny, was wounded in or near Turkey, World War I, died later of shell shock at age 16.

My only child, son Peter, is in the movies. Owing to a serious injury to his right arm as a child, he helps with my apartment rent.

My sister, widow of General Glencairn Campbell, late A & S Highlanders, is now serving in the Women's Army in Rhodesia (Salisbury). Her second husband, General Palmer, is also dead.

I am very poor, my husband having met a depression and lost all his fortune before he died, and I am literally unhappy here— too poor for friends— and I only see my son about once in four years. He married into an Irish family who dislike the British and do not conceal the fact. He is divorced, has four children. All I have as companion is my little cat that I love and that loves me. I pray daily that he will be allowed to come with me because otherwise I am so alone.

Yours sincerely

From: Major R. Mandalay, M.V.O., M.B.E.

        Privy Purse Office
        Buckingham Palace
        25th January 1967

Dear Lady Lawford:

Your letter addressed to Mr. Whitlock has been passed to me, as this Office is responsible for Grace and Favour apartments.

I am very sorry to hear of your present difficulties. It is, therefore, with much regret that I have to write and tell you that, owing to the very long waiting list of ladies requiring accommodation at Hampton Court Palace, we have been obliged to close the list for the time being...

I am sorry to send you such an unfavorable reply, but I am sure you will understand the position.

I return the medical certificate and your photograph herewith.
        Yours sincerely,
        R. Mandalay
        Assistant Keeper
        of the Privy Purse

That's that! Now, just look at some of these Hearst newspaper headlines: *Lady May's Wild Mustang Ride.* They make my accidents sound like publicity stunts. My God, look at those bruises and my ripped lip and nine teeth down my throat! Does that sound like a publicity stunt? Look at all I have gone through— imagine that Sergeant Lewis of the police trying to make me a criminal. I told him, "You're not going to make a bloody hit-and-run out of me." Of course, I told him that— they tried to charge me with hit-and-run driving. Ha!

All I did was let someone take me to the Beverly Hills Emergency Clinic— I was holding my lip in my hand— didn't the doctor do a beautiful job of sewing me up? That awful clinic— nothing but niggers— how awful. Little wonder I tore up that name card. Thank God for my own doctor who took a needle and thread and sewed me up so beautifully.

I no sooner returned to my drawing room than some officer put his finger under my chin like this and said, "Be a good little citizen. Come on and tell me how old you are?"

"I'm not a Yank," I said, "I don't have to tell you a bloody thing. I'm a British subject and immune." I'm sure I said more, but they were things I'd prefer not to think about.

Insurance— I never heard a word about insurance. No one said a word about insurance— especially that salesman Franks who took everything in my house that the nurse or the maid had not already taken. You remember when Herbert Hischemoeller made that Franks give him all the things he took from me?

Look at this amusing article written about me in this week's *Sports Illustrated* or some magazine like that. Imagine me in one of *those* magazines! The article is absurd but amusing:

> Los Angeles residents who lack the time or money to make it out to Indy for the 500 this month might just go and stand around Lady May Lawford's garage, because Actor Peter Lawford's mother (74 according to Los Angeles Times clippings, 66 by her own reckoning) is where the action is. On April 1, salesman Robert D. Franks sold Lady Lawford a convertible Ford Fairlane G.T. On April 5, she backed it out of her

driveway at 40 mph— across the street, over a sapling and into a parked car. It was an exciting performance but, dissatisfied, Lady Lawford shot forward with undiminished speed into the concrete wall of her garage. The car was a total loss and so might have been a lesser woman than Peter's mother, who had to have nine teeth surgically removed from the back of her throat. She was still under her doctor's care on May 10th, when salesman Franks brought over a shiny, brand-new, six-cylinder Ford Mustang. On May 11, Lady Lawford backed the Mustang— at 40 mph— out of the garage and into the house across the street and then roared into Frank's parked car. Damage to house across the street: $700. Damage to Mustang: $1500. Damage to Mr. Frank's car:$1000. Damage to Lady Lawford: negligible. She is feeling very well, thank you, but is thinking of giving up driving.

Dear Mr. Phillips:
This is the situation on the first car. I came down thesteps. Mr. Franks, the salesman, showed me the car (in No. 7 garage), said, "Good morning" *only* (no word of insurance, etc.), and I put it in gear in what was marked "Reverse." It took off at about 40 mph backwards and it almost killed me, the accelerator appears to "have stuck." (I tried it.)
Word came from Head Salesman Mr. Franks that Ford, etc. would replace the first car with another because of "faulty accelerator." Unquote...
On May 10, the salesman delivered the second car and, when I descended the steps, he said, "Good morning!" and "The car is in garage No. 7." Unquote. *No mention was*   made to me by anyone about insurance of the car that replaced the defective one— no one from Ford's office or anywhere phoned me about insurance or told me when they saw me. He let me take over and you know the rest. The mark on the console on the Mustang was at No. 2 and I noticed it as I put my foot on the accelerator (too late to stop). It also took off backwards at about 40 mph at least! The rest you know.
I have driven all types and makes of cars from Rolls Royces to Model T to Cadillac, Hispano‑Swizu, Argyll-Sunbeam, etc. all over the world. My first car at age sixteen was given me by my father (if and when I passed the Army test). Having lived in India, Burma, China, Ceylon, Australia, Lisbon, London, Dublin, Paris, Rome, Tahiti, Hong Kong, Monte Carlo, Nice, etc., etc. The fact that I am a novice as regards to driving cars is absurd.
I am prepared to swear in any court on a stack of Bibles that what I have written is the truth.
Yours sincerely, Lady May Lawford

Oh, what is to become of me? One car with a stuck accelerator,

maybe. But *another* new car with a "faulty accelerator"? Impossible!
Please God, please watch after me! Please!

Buddie dear:
Must see you tomorrow. Have decided. Monte Carlo.At once. Karen,
Dr. Ellis— Peter, etc., all visited me and told me Peter wanted me in a
"nursing home"— Nurses round the clock.
The story when we meet— must be tomorrow. Might go next day or
Sunday! Full of ideas— cannot stick. Doctor is full of bull!!
Love and lots of it,
May.

Afterword

By
Buddy Galon

Lady Lawford was murdered. It was just as simple as that. No one put a gun to her head and no one squeezed a trigger. But she died as a result of what was done to her.

***

While I was on a business trip away from California, Lady Lawford and I were in constant communications. She complained about my absence (she always felt a void when I was away). I always asked about her health, and she proudly reported it was excellent, except for her minor arthritis in her second and third fingers of each hand. However, no other ailments— Dr. Gundersen, her doctor whom she jokingly called the "Society Stallion", confirmed this. She talked about Peter's drinking, and griped about the new Arab neighbors who played a "tin penny whistle" during the night that kept her awake. I assured her that I would check into this upon my return.

On my next business stop, I, as usual, called her. There was no answer. When I called her a second time and got no answer, I began to worry, and worried to the very end of my trip because I was not able to reach her.

With a couple of gifts tucked away in my luggage, and a thought about a candlelight dinner with Lady Lawford, I decided to stop by my Hollywood office to pick up my mail. There I found her special delivery letter:

"Buddie dear:
Must see you tomorrow. Have decided. Monte Carlo. At once. Karen, Dr. Ellis— Peter, etc., all visited me and told me Peter *wanted* me in a "nursing home"— round the clock.
The story when we meet— *must be tomorrow.* Might go next day or Sunday! Full of ideas— cannot stick. Doctor is full of bull!!
Love and lots of it,
May

Karen was a well-meaning secretary of the production company; Dr. Ellis was an easily-led physician who sometimes treated Lady Lawford for her minor arthritis pains; her son Peter, "etc." usually meant the manager and the lawyer; "all visited me", must have been some summit meeting! "and told me Peter *wanted* me in a "nursing home"— nurses round the clock". Lady Lawford placed quotation marks on either side of Peter's idea of a "nursing home"— meaning a locked facility with nurses dispensing medication...
"Love and lots of it, May".
I dashed to the telephone to call her and found her telephone was disconnected. I ran to my car and raced to the apartment.
"May, I'm here! May, I'm here!" I shouted. "Everything's going to be all right." I banged on the door, and dipped into my pocket for my door key. On pushing the door, I saw only bare rooms. "Oh God, I'm too late!" I exclaimed, tears streaming down my face.
Days passed by without my finding any trace of her. The nervous "Arab" neighbor, who played the noisy tin penny whistle, reluctantly admitted seeing men "carry away" her British neighbor who appeared to be "sleeping".
I called Dr. Ellis, but got no information. Even the police and FBI rebuffed me. Then I turned to Patrick Mahony and Baron Herbert von Hischemoeller to help me find our mutual friend.
Unable to get any clue whatsoever, I began to fear for her life. I asked others to help: Richard Brian, Zee Gee Jordan, Thelma Keaton,

Charles Whitewolf, Peter Dane, Marguerite Place, Lori Lane, Eleanor Powell, and even Beulah Bondi— all efforts to no avail.

Then one night, nearly six months later, while with friends in a Beverly Hills discotheque, my attention was drawn to a rather loud, blustery man hanging on to the bar. His boasting remarks becoming boring, I prepared to move away when the braggart unexpectedly said, "I'm a hospital administrator and I've got Peter Lawford's mother, Lady Lawford, hidden away."

I bought the windbag a couple of drinks in hopes of further loosening his tongue. Feigning great interest, I asked him all about his interesting line of work. Finally, he told me the street of the hospital where he worked.

The next day I drove for about thirty-five miles until I found the street and the "rest home". I wandered freely in the halls looking in each room. As I proceeded down the hall, this black woman stopped me.

"Come to see your grandmother? Well, which one is she? What's her name?" That was all I needed to hear. When I said "Lawford", she registered surprise. Then, lowering her voice to a whisper, she told me that no one except my Daddy and the Doctor was supposed to know Lady Lawford was there. But since Peter Lawford was my dad, she would take me to see my grandmother.

Lady Lawford sat motionless in a chair. I did not recognize her at first. Only her distinctive nose, her flawless complexion, and her unusual upper lip line made me positive that this stooped figure was the object of my long search. More than fifty pounds of weight loss left her the appearance of a Nazi concentration camp victim. The fact that her uncolored hair had been literally hacked— not cut, to a three inch length all over her head added to the prisoner of war comparison. A thin muslin shift (which I later learned had been removed from a corpse only the day before) barely covered her emaciated body. One breast was exposed and even her private area could be seen. The lower front of her white shift was wet where her urine had bathed it and trickled onto the floor beneath her chair forming a yellow pool. The back of her shift was stuck to her with human excrement, and on the back of her legs was dried fecal matter. Restraints imprisoned her at her ankles, at her waist, at her wrists and even at her mouth. Her dazed eyes did not blink; they did not move noticeably at any time.

When her mouth restraint was removed, she did not utter one sound. At no time did Lady Lawford show any recognition of me. I could not believe what I was seeing.

Gone was the real Lady Lawford: her erect, regal bearing, the long dark auburn hair perfectly groomed in an upswept style, her fastidious cleanliness and meticulous grooming— (she would not come to breakfast until completing her bath, making up her face, slipping into a black dress, and putting on her pearls); gone was the twinkle in her ever-alert eyes; gone were the ready smile and her distinctive British accent. Gone was the real Lady Lawford.

How could they have done this to her?

Seeing me in near despair, the nurse confided in me that Lady Lawford was brought in nearly dead from a massive drug overdose. She told me that the evening of her admittance, the doctor, the hospital administrator, and two attendants carried the comatose Lady Lawford to her room. When she told that, in her opinion, Lady Lawford's condition would never improve, my heart seemed to skip a beat.

Unbeknown to anyone, and with the help of the nurse, for many hopeless months I played the dual role of speech therapist and exercise therapist. My efforts paid off when she said her first word and managed to take a few steps. Our efforts were shortlived because a few nights later Lady Lawford stumbled on her chair and broke a bone in her leg.

The   doctor, who had been avoiding talking with me   he seemed to know too much and did not want to risk knowing I was around, finally asked me to get Peter Lawford's permission for surgery. I immediately got to work and traced Peter in Puerta Vallarta. With the doctor and me on the conference telephone hook-up, the boozing *son* spurted: "Why don't you just shoot her in the goddamned leg and be done with it! Now leave me alone— I'm getting married."

With that, the doctor doubled the dosage and Lady Lawford never again uttered a word or touched the floor.

The doctor finally admitted his role in Lady Lawford's planned demise. He told me that, with the exception of arthritis in her fingers, she was in excellent health— such good health that she did not even succumb to the massive drug overdose. "She has the constitution of a horse!" he exclaimed.

Wanting him to tell more, I asked him to go to dinner with me and to go see a movie (a motion picture supposedly based on my relationship with Lady Lawford). He called saying that he would meet me for the engagement in thirty minutes. He never showed up. His unmarked body was found face down on the kitchen floor in a totally unexplained death. His pan of Campbell's tomato soup had boiled dry.

***

A few days later, on returning to the "rest home", I learned that Lady Lawford had died. Though I knew this was bound to happen soon, I still could not believe or accept it. I asked the whereabouts of her body, but no one was able to give me any information.

A laborious hunt through the many mortuaries of Los Angeles finally led to a funeral home in North Hollywood. On asking why she had been taken there, the spokesman replied matter-of-fact that it had been the decision of her son and that of the doctor. When I asked to see her, the same person told me that Lady Lawford had already been cremated. "But she hasn't even been dead six hours!" I exclaimed, knowing that Lady Lawford did not wish to be cremated— she wished to have a simple funeral service at St. Alban's Church in Westwood and her body buried afterwards at Westwood Memorial Park. When I asked about services, the man told me that the office of Peter Lawford's Chrislaw Productions had announced there would be no services. That is one thing I would not allow.

When I learned that there was not going to be any services, I moved full-steem ahead and, totally undaunted, arranged to hold a memorial service for Lady Lawford. I notified Peter of the service, telling his office that I had chosen St. Alban's church for Friday evening at 7:30 PM, and telephoned more than twenty-five of Lady Lawford's and my closest friends. I, even telegraphed messages to her grandchildren as well as notifying the press. Two days later, a spokesman for Peter announced to the press that he would be in charge of the service to be held at the same church, same date and same time. Nevertheless, we all attended and were appalled with the inappropriate clergymen, floral displays, and sacred music. Dressed in a tweed sport coat, Peter sat down front with his wife Mary Ann Rowan, both of whom studied me carefully as I sat opposite them in the front pew.

The death of Lady Lawford ironically marked her son's plummeting descent, never to rise again. Unending bouts with alcoholism, interrupted only by brief and lengthy periods of hospitalization, dogged him until the end of his life. His flagging acting career almost became nonexistent, and his family relations nearly at a standstill. No friends filled his waking hours. There were whispers of AIDS and homosexuality fueled by his continued drug habit. Surely his emaciated and haggard appearance made many people wonder, and with good reason.

When doctors told Peter that he only had hours to live, he married Patricia Seaton, thirty-five years his junior— only she knows the reasons for that last-minute marriage.

Upon seeing Peter in those conditions, Elizabeth Taylor convinced him to join her in treatment at the Betty Ford Center for alcohol and drug abuse. She even got him a small part in her television movie, *Malice in Wonderland* where on the set, Peter collapsed and was taken to the UCLA medical center. He died there on Christmas Eve, 1984.

Cremated, Peter's ashes were buried at Westwood Memorial Park just as he requested. Supposedly Elizabeth Taylor paid the funeral expenses; Jackie Kennedy Onassis purportedly withdrew funds from the Kennedy Foundation to help defray the costs. Neither Patricia Kennedy Lawford nor the four Lawford children were present at the services. Newspapers reported them vacationing in Jamaica.

Born with a silver spoon in his mouth, his mother gave him all: aristocratic birth; Oxford tutoring; homes in London, Paris, India, Majorca, Monte Carlo, Tahiti, Honolulu, Australia, Palm Beach, and Beverly Hills; a fourteen-year contract with M-G-M, and a social atmosphere where he could meet princesses and ambassadors' daughters. Most of all, she gave him deep and undying love— regardless of what she may have said about him.   Having spent millions supporting his alcohol-drug life style; at death he owned no house, no real estate, no stocks and bonds; he did not even have a bank account. Lady Lawford's son died having no wealth, no home, no friends, no money, no family, and worse of all, no love, unlike his mother, who had and continues to have both my undying love and deepest respect.

Photographs
and
Commentaries

1. Lady Lawford— a typical pose with fur, jewels, and *acid* tongue.

2. Lady Lawford— "my favorite picture of me"— this photograph is often seen with her published writings.

3.Military hero Sir Sydney Turing Barlow Lawford— "The General and my distinguished husband."

4. King George I and Queen Mary represented the dignified royalty in which Lady Lawford so staunchly believed. King George knighted General Lawford in 1918, and the royal couple remained close friends with him.

5. Seeing the drunken Prince of Wales playing polo, Lady Lawford
insisted her husband "pull rank, for God's sake!" forcing the future
King of England to dismount.

6. Ambassador Joseph Kennedy (left) with Gloria Swanson's husband Marquis le Bailly de la Falaise de La Coudraye. Although the Marquis and Rose suffered in silence during their mates' long affair, Lady Lawford protested, "I wouldn't have kept *my* mouth shut!"

7. Glamorous Gloria Swanson (age 80) "set up housekeeping with Old Joe both at a 56th St. New York apartment and a California mansion opposite the Beverly Hills Hotel— the first house there with an elevator. She even named her son Joseph Patrick after Old Kennedy!"

8. "Those barefoot Irish peasants! Do they really think that they are like the British Royal Family just because they are called 'The First Lady'? I must say, however, that they have done well as a family."

9. In *Son of Lassie* Peter's screen career continued to soar in spite of his Lord Jeff co-star Freddie Bartholomew's attempt to expose a deep secret of the Lawford's family.

10. Actor Peter Lawford— "How could the handsome lad I so carefully brought up turn into such an awful brat? But I love him."

11. Peter's handsomeness, quick wit, and general ability opened the door to romance, sociability, and film employment in his early years. At the first sign of being seduced by fame, Sir Sydney Lawford told his son, "You're not taking all of this too seriously, are you? You know, it can be taken away as quickly as it was given."

12. "Before Peter married Patricia Kennedy, both the ambassador's daughter Sharman Douglas and Princess Ira von Furstenberg threw themselves at him."

13. Patricia Kennedy, who Lady Lawford referred to as "Miss Kennedy" before, during, and after her marriage to Peter, was bound by "the hold Joseph Kennedy had exercised over his daughters." Peter said, "I always felt that her love for her father took precedence over her love for me." (Pictured here with her brother JFK and Peter)

14. Patricia Kennedy Lawford ended twelve years of marriage to Peter in a twelve-minute divorce hearing in Idaho. "Good riddance! I am more than happy to have nothing to do with any of the Kennedys in any way in the future, as sorry as I am about my grandchildren."

15. Teddy Kennedy (left) and brother-in-law Peter in an early Palm Beach photo. Did Teddy suspect Lady Lawford of revealing to the press a secret of his cheating and subsequent expulsion from Harvard? Her reason was retaliation against the Kennedys because, she said, they prevented her from seeing her grandchildren.

16. President John F. Kennedy was a close friend to his brother-in-law Peter. Both Jack and brother Bobby used Peter for introductions to glamorous women and for the use of his beach house. "I liked Jack, but his mind was always on his cock."

17. Marilyn Monroe, only days before her death, poses— with her ever-present glass of champagne— for her last photograph at Peter's beach house.

18. A publicity picture of Peter, who survived in his acting career child-star parts, juvenile roles, hearthrob characters, and then supporting actor. This photo is personally autographed, but usually he snubbed his fans' requests. Lady Lawford admonished him openly: "You owe it to them to grant them autographs."

19. With this stern face, Lady Lawford co-starred with Ronald Reagan and Rhonda Fleming in the motion picture *Hong Kong*.

20. Lady Lawford maintained her aristocratic elegance when she appeared in the movie, *Mr. Peabody and the Mermaid* with William Powell and Ann Blythe.

21. Lady Lawford (with Peter's manager Milton Ebbins and Peter) prepares for "The Thin Man" television series appearance. "Once, I was on Peter's 'Thin Man' show. It was a ball!... But after Peter joined the 'royal family', they didn't want me to act."

22. Under the professional name of Mary Sommerville (her real name), Lady Lawford appeared in several films. Her pronunciation of "Worsterchershire sauce" opened the door to commercials for her.

23. *Suave, debonair, dashing, savoir faire, bonvivant* are all terms used to describe Peter and his image. Seldon was his intellect and intelligence recognized— Did you know that he holds the all-time record for winning the television quiz show *Password?*

24. In the 1974 production of *That's Entertainment* (which Lady Lawford did not live to see) Peter appeared in his last movie hit. Alcohol and drugs were already taking their toll.

25. Reduced from supporting roles to bit and cameo parts, Peter had to admit that his appearance suffered from his self-destructive life style. When a producer turned him down for a role because fo age, Peter asked, "What happened to that time when I'd be perfect?" The producer answered, "I guess it just went by."

26. Weakened by the loss of weight and loss of blood, and ravaged by a lifetime of heavy drinking and drug use, Peter was dying when old friend Elizabeth Taylor inisted that he join her for treatment at the Betty Ford Center for Alcohol and Drug Abuse.

27. Princess Franz Friedrich zu Hohenlohe Waldenburg Schilling-sfurst— "I called her 'Steph'— has always been a dear friend. Thank heavens she helped me get through that awful fiasco called Patricia and Peter's wedding! For years people have accused Steph of being Hitler's girlfriend, but I don't care— I adore her!"

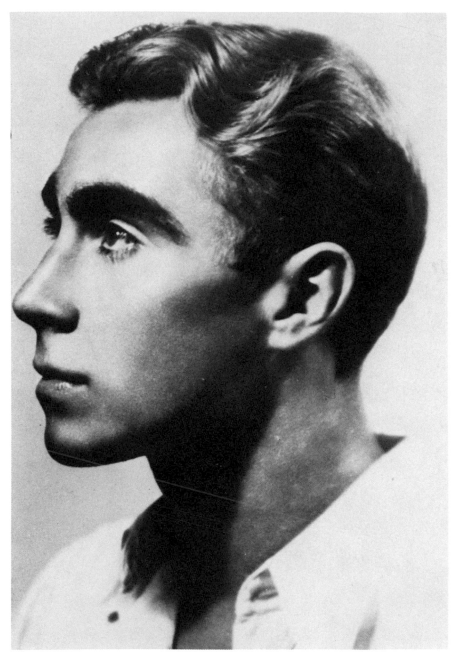

28. "Ah, my wonderful Franzi— he's really Steph's son. Prince
Franz Hohenlohe— is such a darling! He can fence; he can row; he
can swim— what a physique! And what a marvelous host!"

29. Lady Lawford— The One and Only!

Index Of Names

Photo Credits

(Photo by Lori Lane)

The author stands in front of the suspended staircase at his family's ancestral home.

Woburn Abbey, outside of London, has been the residence of the Dukes of Bedford for 300 years.

Buddy Galon

Buddy Galon, who has maintained residences in Beverly Hills, Palm Springs, and Palm Beach, is equally at home in the company of royalty, nobility, world leaders, or the greats of Hollywood. During his doctoral studies at UCLA, as well as Oxford University in England and at the Sorbonne in Paris, he wrote a Hollywood gossip column and an educational history of Palm Springs. Buddy Galon's diversity knows no boundaries: from child performer to President Reagan's inaugural entertainer; from filmdom's youth minister to celebrity talk show host on television; from head of the theatre arts department in America's largest private school system to stage, television, and motion picture director; and finally, from the youngest inclusion in *Who's Who in American Music* to the writing of *Bitch, The Autobiography of Lady Lawford.*